AF266857

Norse Mythology for Beginners

The Tales of the Vikings Simplified for People Who Slept Through History Class

Free Bonus from Captivating History (Available for a Limited time)

Hi History Lovers!

Now you have a chance to join our exclusive history list so you can get your first history ebook for free as well as discounts and a potential to get more history books for free!

Simply visit the link below to join.

Or, Scan the QR code!

captivatinghistory.com/ebook

Also, make sure to follow us on Facebook, X, and YouTube by searching for Captivating History.

Table of Contents

Introduction: Why the Vikings Still Matter

If you think you know Norse mythology, you probably don't. Or at least, you don't know the real version.

You've seen Thor in the movies, swinging his hammer and cracking jokes with his Avenger buddies. You've probably heard about Valhalla, where Viking warriors feast forever after dying gloriously in battle. And if you've ever been to a Halloween party, you've likely seen someone wearing a horned helmet and claiming it's "Viking."

But that right there is the problem. Much of what you think you know is simplified, exaggerated, or just plain wrong.

The Vikings never wore horned helmets; that myth came from 19th-century opera costumes. Archaeological evidence shows Viking helmets were simple iron caps designed to keep the skull intact during a sword fight. This alone reveals something important. Norse mythology has been filtered and Hollywood-ized so many times that the original barely resembles what survives today. The real myths are actually stranger, darker, and far more interesting than anything Marvel has produced.

The Vikings didn't have a sacred book. They had stories, passed down orally for generations and memorized by poets called skalds. By the time Christian scholars in Iceland recorded these myths in the 13th century, the old religion was dying. What survived was essentially a rescue operation, with monks and scholars trying to save stories they no longer believed.

That's why Norse mythology feels incomplete. There are gaps, contradictions, and frustrating moments where you can tell something important is missing. The sources we have, the *Prose Edda* and the *Poetic Edda*, are like finding half a puzzle. You can see the picture, but you're left wondering what the missing pieces showed.

Still, what remains is remarkable. These are myths about gods who bleed, lie, and make catastrophic mistakes. They're stories about a universe held together by a giant tree, where squirrels carry insults between dragons and eagles, and where the entire cosmos was built from the body parts of a murdered giant. This is mythology where the heroes know they're doomed, where fate cannot be escaped, and where even the gods will die when the world ends.

Unlike the immortal gods of many other religions, the Norse gods live under the shadow of Ragnarök, the prophesied end of everything. They know it's coming, and they know they'll lose. Yet they keep fighting anyway. That worldview, facing certain doom with courage and dignity, tells you everything you need to know about the people who believed these stories.

The Norse concept of fate, which they called *urðr* or *ørlög* (related to the Old English *wyrd*, which became our modern word "weird"), wasn't quite the same as fate in Greek or Roman mythology. This was more like a web of cause and effect, where past actions created present circumstances that shaped future outcomes. You couldn't escape your fate, but how you faced it defined your honor. For a Viking warrior, dying well mattered more than living a long life. The worst thing you could be was a *níðingr*, a person without honor, someone who broke oaths or acted with cowardice.

This obsession with honor helps explain why Vikings carved their deeds into runestones and risked everything on voyages across the North Atlantic. If people remembered your name and told your story, you achieved a kind of immortality that was more valuable than any heaven.

The myths reflected these values. When Loki causes the death of Baldr, the most beloved god, the punishment is brutal. When the wolf Fenrir is bound through trickery, the god Týr sacrifices his hand to make it happen, accepting permanent mutilation as the price of keeping his oath. When Thor faces impossible challenges in a giant's hall, he learns that even gods can be humbled.

These aren't children's stories, though they have been sanitized into children's books. The original myths include graphic violence, sexual content, and moral ambiguity that would make modern parents uncomfortable. Gods seduce giants, transform into animals to mate with other animals, and slaughter enemies with gleeful brutality. Dwarves are murdered for their treasures. Humans are created as an afterthought from driftwood. The universe begins with heat and ice, creating a cosmic cow who licks a god out of salty ice.

It's bizarre. It's violent. It's frequently uncomfortable. And it's absolutely fascinating.

This book will take you through the real Norse myths as they appear in the medieval sources. We'll start at the beginning with a void called Ginnungagap and the first giant born from melting ice. We'll meet the gods in their halls, explore the Nine Worlds connected by the World Tree, and witness the friendships, rivalries, and feuds that shape the cosmos. We'll see dwarves forge magical weapons, watch Thor dress in drag to infiltrate a giant's wedding, and follow Odin as he sacrifices everything, even himself, for wisdom and power.

And we'll end where the Vikings knew their world would end: with fire, flood, and the death of the gods and giants alike. This was followed by a quiet rebirth and the faint hope that something better might grow from the ashes.

These stories survived against incredible odds. They deserve to be told properly, in all their strange, violent, complicated glory. So forget the horned helmets, set aside what Marvel taught you, and let's dive into the actual myths of the North.

The Cheat Sheet:
A Who's Who of the Nine Worlds

Before we dive in, here's a quick reference guide to keep everyone straight. Norse mythology has a lot of characters, and they're all related to each other in ways that would make a soap opera seem simple.

The Big Three

Odin: King of the gods, obsessed with knowledge, gave up an eye for wisdom, and hanged himself from a tree for nine days to discover runes. Father of many gods and some humans. Owns an eight-legged horse and two ravens that spy for him.

Thor: Odin's son, god of thunder, protector of humanity, owner of the hammer Mjölnir. Strong, brave, straightforward, with a legendary temper. Prefers direct action over clever schemes. The most popular god among Vikings.

Loki: Blood brother to Odin, father of monsters, trickster, shapeshifter, and the reason everything eventually goes wrong. Helpful one day, catastrophic the next. Gave birth to an eight-legged horse—yes, really.

Other Important Gods

Frigg: Odin's wife, queen of the gods, knows everyone's fate but rarely reveals it.

Baldr: Son of Odin and Frigg, most beautiful and beloved of all gods. His death triggers Ragnarök.

Týr: God of war and justice, sacrificed his hand to bind the wolf Fenrir.

Heimdall: Watchman of the gods, guards the rainbow bridge, will blow his horn when Ragnarök begins.

Freyja: Goddess of love, beauty, fertility, and war. Gets first pick of slain warriors before Odin.

Freyr: Freyja's twin brother, god of fertility and prosperity, will die at Ragnarök because he traded his sword for a wife.

The Monsters (Loki's Children)

Fenrir: A wolf so large and terrible that it takes all the gods working together to bind him.

Jörmungandr: The World Serpent, a snake so massive it encircles the entire earth and bites its own tail.

Hel: Half alive, half corpse, rules over the realm of the dead who didn't die in battle.

The Nine Worlds:

The sources never give us a definitive, complete list of the Nine Worlds. What we can do is reconstruct them based on various references in the Eddas and other texts. Scholars have pieced together this framework, but the original Norse believers might have organized things differently.

Asgard: Home of the gods, connected to Midgard by the rainbow bridge Bifrost.

Midgard: Earth, home of humans, literally "Middle Earth" or "Middle Enclosure."

Jötunheim: Land of the giants, often in conflict with the gods but not always.

Vanaheim: Home of the Vanir gods (Freyr, Freyja, and Njörðr), associated with fertility and prosperity.

Helheim: The realm of the dead, ruled by Hel, cold and misty.

Niflheim: Realm of ice and mist, existed before creation.

Muspelheim: Realm of fire, also primordial, home to fire giants.

Álfheim: Home of the light elves.

Svartálfheim: Home of the dark elves and dwarves (master craftsmen who live underground). In the sources, dark elves and dwarves may actually be the same beings.

Pronunciation Guide: A Quick Reference

Old Norse pronunciation can be tricky, but you don't need to be perfect. Here's a practical guide to the names and terms you'll encounter most often. When in doubt, just do your best; even scholars disagree on some of these.

The Basics

J sounds like the English Y (Jötunheim = "YOH-tun-haym")

Ð/ð (eth) sounds like TH in "the" (Urðr = "OORTH")

Þ/þ (thorn) sounds like TH in "think" (Þrúðr = "THROOTH")

R is always rolled

Stress usually falls on the first syllable

Major Names

Gods and Beings

Odin = OH-din

Thor = THOR (like you'd expect)

Loki = LOH-kee

Freyja = FRAY-uh

Freyr = FRAYR ("fray" with a light R at the end—it is one syllable)

Baldr = BALD-ur

Týr = TEER

Heimdall = HAYM-dahl

Frigg = FRIG

Hel = HEL

Giants and Monsters:

Ymir = EE-mir

Fenrir = FEN-reer

Jörmungandr = YOR-mun-gand-ur

Níðhöggr = NEETH-hog-ur

Surtr = SURT-ur

Places:

Asgard = AHS-guard

Midgard = MID-guard

Jötunheim = YOH-tun-haym

Niflheim = NIF-ul-haym

Muspelheim = MUS-pell-haym

Vanaheim = VAH-nah-haym

Álfheim = AHLF-haym

Svartálfheim = SVART-ahlf-haym

Helheim = HEL-haym

Yggdrasil = IG-drah-sill

Bifrost = BEE-frost or vrost

Valhalla = val-HAHL-ah (or val-HAL-uh)

Concepts and Things:

Mjölnir = MYOHL-neer (Thor's hammer)

Gungnir = GOONG-neer (Odin's spear)

Ginnungagap = GIN-nung-ah-gap

Ragnarök = RAG-nah-rok

Urðr = OORTH (also spelled Urd)

Jötnar = YOT-nar (giants, plural)

Jötunn = YO-tun (giant, singular)

Æsir = EYE-seer (the main tribe of gods)

Vanir = VAH-neer (the other tribe of gods)

Einherjar = AYN-hair-yar (Odin's chosen warriors)

Common Terms:

Wyrd = WEIRD (fate, Old English, not Old Norse)

Urðr/Ørlög = OORTH/UR-log (fate, Old Norse versions)

Seiðr = SAY-thur (magic)

Skald = SKALD (poet)

Níðingr = NEETH-ing-ur (person without honor)

Don't stress too much about perfect pronunciation. The important thing is understanding the stories and the world they describe. Even Vikings from different regions probably pronounced these names differently.

Chapter 1: The Blueprint of the Universe

Ginnungagap: The Great Nothing

In the beginning, there was nothing. Not the philosophical kind of nothing that keeps you awake at 3 a.m. wondering about existence. We're talking about a vast, undefined gap between realms that didn't exist yet, a void called Ginnungagap.

The word itself is Old Norse for something like "yawning gap" or "gaping abyss," which gives you a sense of the scale we're dealing with. This wasn't empty space waiting to be filled. This was a primordial gap, a space of potential between opposing forces.

But Ginnungagap wasn't entirely alone in the primordial void. To the north lay Niflheim, a realm of ice, mist, and freezing fog. In later interpretations, this realm came to represent the ultimate absence of warmth, a place where even thought seemed to freeze and shatter. Eleven rivers called the Élivágar flowed from a spring named Hvergelmir in the heart of Niflheim. Their names were preserved in the sources: Svöl, Gunnþrá, Fjörm, Fimbulþul, Slíðr, Hríð, Sylgr, Ylgr, Víð, Leiptr, and Gjöll.

These weren't pleasant babbling brooks. The waters were eitr-filled (venomous). As they flowed away from their source, layer upon layer of ice built up. The venom in the water hardened into rime, and this rime accumulated over countless ages, creeping slowly toward the center of Ginnungagap like glaciers made of frozen poison.

To the south existed Muspelheim, a realm of fire and heat that was equally extreme. Where Niflheim was cold and dark, Muspelheim blazed with flames that never dimmed and heat that never subsided. Later traditions described this as elemental fire in its purest form, the kind of heat that existed before the sun, before stars, before anything that could burn. A giant named Surtr guarded this realm with a flaming sword. He had stood watch since before the world began. He'll show up again at the end of everything, leading armies of fire to consume the cosmos.

For now, what matters is that Muspelheim sent sparks and rivers of molten fire flowing toward Ginnungagap from the opposite direction.

The sources don't explain where Niflheim and Muspelheim came from. They simply existed before anything else, eternal opposites waiting to collide. This might frustrate anyone looking for a neat origin story with clear explanations, but Norse mythology rarely provides those. The myths start in the middle of things and leave you to figure out the rest.

What happened next was inevitable. Ice from the north met fire from the south in the center of Ginnungagap. The ice began to melt. Drops of water formed from the thawing ice, and from these drops, life emerged.

This was not plant life or simple organisms. According to the Vikings, the first living thing was actually a giant named Ymir.

Ymir was fundamentally different from anything that would come after. He was born from the meeting of opposites and was enormous beyond comprehension. His very existence changed the nature of Ginnungagap.

Ymir was a hermaphrodite, which means he could reproduce without a partner. While he slept, he began sweating. From the sweat under his left arm, a male and female giant were born at the same time. His legs mated with each other and produced a son with six heads. These were the first of the jötnar, the race of giants that would become both enemies and occasional allies of the gods.

But Ymir wasn't the only thing born from the melting ice.

As more ice thawed in the warmth from Muspelheim, the drops formed into another being. This one was a cow. Her name was Auðumbla, and she was enormous. Four rivers of milk flowed from her udders, which provided nourishment for Ymir and his offspring.

Auðumbla herself was fed by licking the salty ice blocks that filled Ginnungagap. She licked them constantly, and as she did, something remarkable happened. On the first day of licking, hair appeared in the ice.

On the second day, a head emerged. On the third day, an entire man stepped free from the ice.

His name was Búri. The sources tell us he was beautiful, tall, and strong, but they don't explain what he was or where he came from before being frozen in the ice. Was he always there, waiting to be freed? Was he formed by Auðumbla's licking the way Ymir was formed from melting ice? Had he existed in some other form before the ice claimed him? The myths don't say.

What we do know is that Búri had a son named Borr, though we're not told how this happened or who Borr's mother was. Borr married a giantess named Bestla, who was the daughter of a giant named Bölþorn. The name Bölþorn means something like "Evil Thorn," which gives you a sense of his nature.

This marriage between Borr and Bestla is the first example of a pattern that would repeat throughout Norse mythology. The gods and giants were enemies, but they were also family. They married each other, had children, and maintained relationships that were far more complex than simple opposition.

Bestla and Borr had three sons: Odin, Vili, and Vé. Their names are significant. Odin means something like "fury," "inspiration," or "possessed." Vili means "will." Vé means "sacred enclosure" or "temple." Together, the three brothers embodied fury, will, and sacredness, the forces that would reshape the cosmos.

These three brothers would change everything.

The First Murder and World-Building

Odin, Vili, and Vé grew up in a cosmos that consisted of ice, fire, Ymir, his giant offspring, and the primordial cow. It wasn't much of a universe. The giants multiplied and spread, but there was no earth, no sky, no sea—just the void, the ice, the fire, and the beings that crawled out of them.

The brothers decided this situation needed to change. More specifically, they decided Ymir needed to die.

The sources don't provide a motive beyond an implied conflict between the two families. Whatever their reasoning, the three brothers attacked Ymir and killed him.

The amount of blood that poured from Ymir's wounds was catastrophic. It flooded Ginnungagap in a deluge so vast that it drowned nearly all of the giants. Only two giants survived. Bergelmir and his wife escaped by climbing onto a lúðr, which might have been a mill, a boat, or some kind of chest. The sources aren't clear. What matters is that they survived, and from them, the race of giants continued.

But the real work was just beginning.

Odin, Vili, and Vé dragged Ymir's massive corpse to the center of Ginnungagap and began building the world from his body. This wasn't metaphorical—they literally constructed the cosmos from the dead giant.

From his flesh came the earth. From his blood, the seas and lakes. From his bones, mountains. From his teeth and bone fragments, rocks and stones. From his hair, trees and vegetation. From his skull, they formed the sky, positioning four dwarves—Norðri, Suðri, Austri, and Vestri (North, South, East, West)—at the corners to hold it up. From his brains, they made the clouds.

The brothers used Ymir's eyebrows to form a protective barrier around Midgard, the realm they were creating for humanity. This barrier would confine the giants to the outer edges of Jötunheim.

Finally, they dealt with the maggots that had formed in Ymir's flesh as it decomposed. These creatures had been feeding on the corpse. The brothers transformed them into dwarves. *Völuspá*, one of the main poems in the *Poetic Edda*, preserves a long catalog of dwarf names, suggesting just how important these beings were to the Norse. Mótsognir was the first and most powerful, followed by Durinn. Then came Nýi, Niði, Norðri, Suðri, Austri, Vestri, Alþjófr, Dvalinn, Nár, Náinn, and dozens more. Each name had meaning, though many of those meanings are lost to us now.

These dwarves would live beneath the mountains and in the earth. They were master craftsmen who would forge the most powerful weapons and treasures in all the Nine Worlds. They had knowledge of runes and magic, and their skill with metals surpassed even the gods. Later traditions describe many dwarves turning to stone if caught by sunlight, making them creatures of darkness who emerged only at night or stayed deep in their mountain homes.

The universe now had structure. It had land, sea, sky, and the basic geography that would define the cosmos. But it still lacked light.

The brothers took sparks and embers from Muspelheim and flung them into the sky. Some became the stars, fixed points of light scattered across the dome of Ymir's skull. Others became wandering lights, what we would later understand as planets, though the Norse saw them as particularly bright stars that moved across the heavens.

Two of the brightest sparks were given a special purpose. The brothers placed them in chariots that would race across the sky, bringing day and night to the world. One spark became the sun, the other the moon.

Yggdrasil: The World Tree

With the basic structure of the cosmos in place, something else emerged—or perhaps it had always been there. The sources aren't clear on whether Yggdrasil grew after the creation of the world or existed before it. What matters is that Yggdrasil became the axis around which everything else turned.

Yggdrasil was an ash tree, but calling it a tree is like calling the ocean a puddle. This was a cosmic tree that connected all of reality. Its branches stretched above the heavens, its trunk passed through the worlds, and its roots dug deep into the realms below.

The name Yggdrasil means "Odin's Horse" or "the Horse of the Terrible One." Ygg was one of Odin's many names, and *drasil* meant horse. This strange name for a tree comes from the story of how Odin discovered the runes, which we'll get to later. For now, it's enough to know that Odin once hanged himself from Yggdrasil's branches for nine days and nights, riding the tree like a horse (the thing that carried him to the edge of death and back again) to gain forbidden knowledge.

Yggdrasil had three main roots, and each one extended into a different realm. The first root reached into Asgard, the realm of the gods. Beneath this root lay the well of Urðr (often anglicized as Urd and also known as Urðarbrunnr), where the Norns—the weavers of fate—made their home. The well's water was sacred and pure. The Norns drew water from it daily and mixed it with mud from the banks to create a special mixture they poured over Yggdrasil's roots.

This wasn't just any old water. The water from Urðr's well had preservative properties, keeping the great tree healthy despite the constant assault it endured. Everything the water touched became as white as the membrane inside an eggshell.

We'll meet the Norns properly later, but they're worth mentioning now because their work was essential to the cosmos's continued existence. Three sisters—Urðr (Past), Verðandi (Present), and Skuld (Future)—sat by the well and carved runes onto small, thin pieces of wood, determining the fate of every being in all the Nine Worlds. Their work was constant. Even the gods couldn't escape the fate the Norns wove for them.

The second root extended into Jötunheim, the land of the giants. Beneath this root was Mímisbrunnr, or Mímir's well, a source of wisdom and knowledge that surpassed all others. The giant Mímir guarded this well jealously. The water it contained held such profound understanding that a single sip could transform the drinker's comprehension of the universe.

Odin would eventually sacrifice one of his eyes for a single drink from Mímir's well, and even for the All-Father, that price was considered fair. The eye remains in the well, looking up from its depths, a permanent reminder of what Odin paid for wisdom. Mímir himself drank from the well regularly, using the horn Gjallarhorn, though some sources suggest this horn belonged to Heimdall instead.

The third root reached down into Niflheim, the primordial realm of ice and mist. Beneath this root writhed Níðhöggr, a massive dragon or serpent whose name means something like "Malice Striker" or "Curse Striker." Níðhöggr gnawed constantly at Yggdrasil's roots. Near him writhed countless serpents, all feeding on the roots alongside their greater cousin. The sources list some names, including Góinn, Móinn, Grábakr, Grafvölluðr, Ófnir, and Sváfnir—all children of Grafvitnir, a primordial serpent.

The tree itself was under constant threat. As mentioned, Níðhöggr and his serpent kin gnawed from below. Four stags—Dáinn, Dvalinn, Duneyrr, and Duraþrór—also wandered through the branches, eating the leaves and bark. The tree should have died from all this abuse, but it didn't. Yggdrasil endured, always dying and always renewing itself, held between destruction and preservation.

Living in Yggdrasil's branches was an unnamed eagle of enormous size. Some sources suggest this eagle possessed great knowledge and wisdom. Perched between the eagle's eyes sat a hawk named Veðrfölnir, whose name might mean "Storm Pale" or "Wind Bleached." The sources don't explain what the hawk did or why it sat on the eagle's head, but there it was, watching the worlds from the highest point in existence. Perhaps it saw things even the eagle couldn't see, or perhaps it served as the eagle's eyes in some way.

Níðhöggr and the eagle hated each other. However, they couldn't reach each other to fight directly, so they settled for trading insults. A squirrel named Ratatoskr ran up and down Yggdrasil's trunk, carrying insults between the dragon and the eagle.

Yggdrasil also dripped dew from its branches. Some of this dew was so sweet that bees collected it to make honey. Other drops fell into the valleys; later traditions suggest these became the source of rivers. The tree wasn't just a passive structure connecting the worlds. It was actively shaping the cosmos, providing sustenance, water, and pathways between realms.

The gods held their daily assembly at Yggdrasil. They would ride up to the tree and hold court beneath its branches, making decisions and settling disputes. The tree represented order and law, as it prevented the cosmos from collapsing back into chaos.

But Yggdrasil had another quality that made it truly important in Norse mythology: it appears to endure beyond Ragnarök. When the gods died, when the worlds burned, when everything else was destroyed, Yggdrasil would shake and groan, but it is implied to remain standing. After the flames died down and the floods receded, the tree would still be there, ready to support whatever came next.

The Nine Realms Explained

Yggdrasil connected the Nine Worlds. As we mentioned in the introduction, the sources never give us a complete list, so what follows is reconstructed from multiple references scattered across different texts.

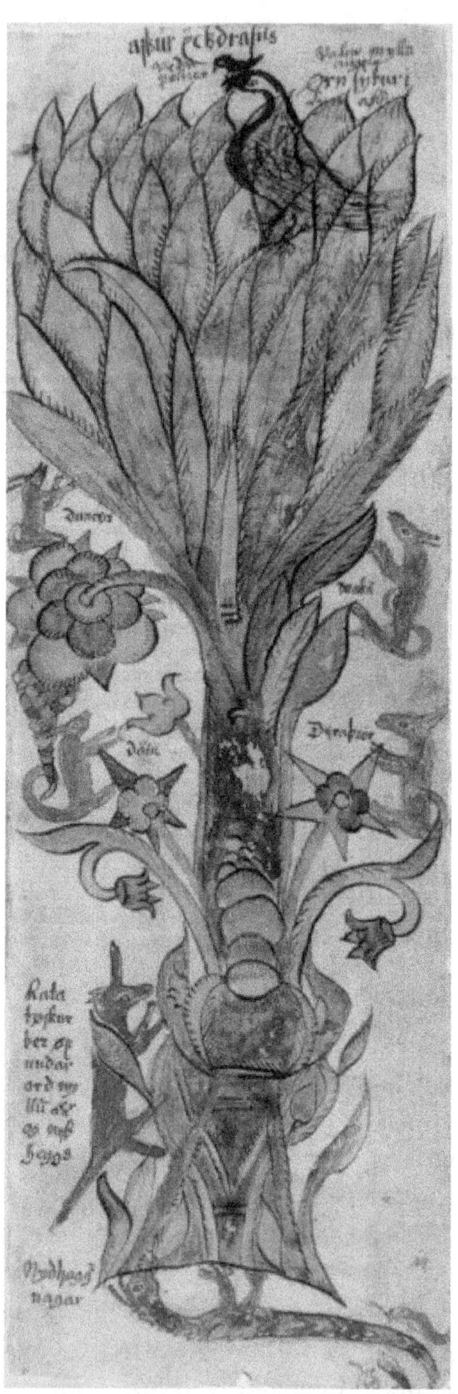

A 17th-century depiction of Yggdrasil.[1]

Asgard sat at the top. It was home to the Æsir gods. This was where Odin had his hall, where Thor kept his hammer, and where Freyja and Freyr lived after coming from the Vanir. Asgard wasn't just one big palace. It contained multiple halls, each belonging to a different god. Odin had Valhalla for his chosen warriors and Valaskjálf, with its high throne from which he could see all the worlds. Thor had Bilskirnir, described as the largest building in existence. Freyja had Fólkvangr, where she took half of those who died in battle.

The gods reached Asgard via the Bifrost, the rainbow bridge that connected their realm to Midgard. The bridge was beautiful, shimmering with colors, but it was also fragile. Heimdall guarded the bridge constantly, watching for giants who might try to invade. The bridge would eventually shatter during Ragnarök when Surtr and his fire giants crossed it to attack Asgard.

Midgard was the realm of humans. It means "Middle Earth," which makes sense since it was positioned in the center of everything. The gods created Midgard from Ymir's body and formed it as a circular disc of land surrounded by ocean. The great World Serpent, Jörmungandr, encircled Midgard in the deep ocean, biting its own tail. The serpent's body formed a barrier between the ordered world of Midgard and the chaos beyond.

Beyond the protective wall the gods had built from Ymir's eyebrows lay the wild, dangerous lands where giants and other hostile forces dwelled. The Vikings who told these stories lived in Midgard, and they understood it as the only truly safe realm.

Jötunheim was the land of the giants, though "giants" is a misleading translation of jötnar. These beings weren't always massive. Some towered over mountains and shook the earth when they walked. But others appeared as normal-sized or even beautiful, making them indistinguishable from gods or humans except for their nature. What made them jötnar was their character as forces outside the divine order. They represented the untamed world beyond civilization. They embodied the raw power of nature that couldn't be controlled or fully tamed.

Jötunheim was harsh and wild, reflecting the nature of its inhabitants. Mountains dominated the landscape, their peaks sharp and unwelcoming. Frozen wastes stretched across vast distances, broken only by dense forests where no paths existed. Rocky terrain made travel difficult, and the weather was unpredictable and often violent. This wasn't a land that invited settlement or cultivation. It was a land that resisted human presence, that reminded anyone who entered that they were guests at best and intruders at worst.

The relationship between gods and giants was complex. They were sometimes enemies, sometimes allies. They could even be family. Thor spent much of his time killing giants, but Odin had a giant for a mother. Freyr fell in love with a giant woman and gave up his sword to marry her.

Vanaheim was home to the Vanir, a separate tribe of gods associated with fertility, prosperity, and nature. The sources tell us very little about what Vanaheim looked like or how it was organized. What we know is that the Vanir once went to war with the Æsir. After the war ended in a stalemate, the two groups exchanged hostages to ensure peace. Njörðr, Freyr, and Freyja came to Asgard as part of this exchange and became part of the Æsir pantheon.

Álfheim belonged to the light elves, called ljósálfar. These beings were beautiful and bright, and they were associated with light and nature. The sources tell us almost nothing else about them. We don't have stories about what the light elves did or how they interacted with gods or humans. Freyr ruled over Álfheim.

Svartálfheim, or Nidavellir, was the realm of the dark elves and dwarves. The sources sometimes treat dark elves (*dökkálfar*) and dwarves as the same beings, but other times, they are distinct groups. What we know for certain is that dwarves lived beneath the mountains, in caves and underground halls, and they were the greatest craftsmen in all the Nine Worlds. They forged Thor's hammer Mjölnir, Odin's spear Gungnir, Freyr's ship Skíðblaðnir, and countless other magical objects.

Dwarves were skilled but dangerous. They didn't like being cheated or tricked, and several stories show what happened to those who tried to swindle them. At the same time, dwarves could be outsmarted, and gods and humans who negotiated carefully could acquire their masterwork creations.

Niflheim was the ancient realm of ice, mist, and cold that existed before creation. After Odin and his brothers built the cosmos from Ymir's body, Niflheim remained as the primordial source of ice and darkness. The spring Hvergelmir bubbled up here, sending forth the poisonous rivers that had once flowed into Ginnungagap. Níðhöggr dwelt in Niflheim, gnawing on Yggdrasil's roots and chewing on the corpses of the dead.

Muspelheim was Niflheim's opposite, the realm of fire that existed before creation. Surtr and his fire giants lived here, waiting for Ragnarök when they would march out to burn the world. The sources tell us almost nothing else about Muspelheim except that it was unbearably hot and that only those born to fire could survive there. It existed as potential energy, heat waiting to be unleashed, fueling the fire that would eventually consume everything.

Helheim was the realm of the dead. It was ruled by Hel, the daughter of Loki. This wasn't quite the same as the Christian hell, though Christian scribes writing down these myths couldn't resist making connections. Helheim was cold and misty, located somewhere in or near Niflheim. Those who died of illness, old age, or accidents went to Helheim. It wasn't necessarily a place of punishment, though it wasn't pleasant either. The dead existed there as pale shadows of their living selves, dwelling in a realm of fog and cold.

The distinction between Helheim and other afterlives is important. Warriors chosen by the Valkyries went to Valhalla or Fólkvangr. Those who drowned at sea might go to the goddess Rán's hall beneath the waves. However, most people—farmers, children, the elderly, and anyone who didn't die gloriously in battle—went to Hel's realm. This wasn't about morality or virtue. It was about the manner of your death.

The Nine Worlds were connected by Yggdrasil and separated by boundaries that could sometimes be crossed. The tree provided pathways, though not everyone could use them. Gods could travel along its trunk and branches, moving between worlds through methods the sources don't fully explain. Perhaps certain places along the tree served as gateways. Perhaps knowing the right path was enough.

But there were other ways to travel between realms. The Bifrost, the rainbow bridge, connected Asgard to Midgard, providing a physical path that could be crossed by those permitted to use it. The bridge shimmered with red, blue, and green, though descriptions varied. It was beautiful to look at but also perilous. The bridge was strong enough to support gods and their chosen dead, but it would burn anyone unworthy who tried to cross.

Heimdall, the watchman of the gods, stood guard at the Asgard end of Bifrost. He needed less sleep than a bird, could see for hundreds of miles in any direction, and could hear grass growing. Nothing crossed that bridge without Heimdall knowing about it. He carried the horn

Gjallarhorn, though, as mentioned earlier, some sources confusingly connect this horn to Mimir's well. When Ragnarök arrived, he would blow his horn to summon the gods to their final battle.

Gods traveled to Jötunheim regularly, to fight, negotiate, court giant women, or seek wisdom from giant seers. Giants occasionally visited Asgard, usually through trickery or disguise, though some came as invited guests. Humans might encounter dwarves emerging from their underground halls at night, catch glimpses of elves in deep forests, or stumble into areas where the boundaries between the worlds grew thin. The cosmos was not a collection of sealed boxes but an interconnected web where the boundaries could be navigated by those who knew the way or were brave enough to try.

The Arrival of Humanity

With the worlds created and organized, one major element was still missing: humans. Midgard existed, but no one lived there yet. The gods had built a realm for humanity without actually creating humanity itself.

That changed when three gods—Odin, Hœnir, and Lóðurr—were walking along a beach. Some sources identify Hœnir and Lóðurr as Odin's brothers Vili and Vé under different names. Others treat them as gods who rarely appear in other myths. Regardless of who exactly they were, these three gods found two pieces of driftwood lying on the shore.

The wood wasn't anything special. They were just logs, worn smooth by the sea, stripped of bark, and bleached by salt and sun. But the gods saw potential.

They took the two pieces of wood and carved them into human form. One became a man, the other a woman. But they were still just wood, lifeless and empty. So, each god contributed something to bring them to life.

Odin gave them breath and spirit. Hœnir gave them understanding and movement. They could now think, reason, and make decisions. They could walk, work, and interact with the world around them. Lóðurr gave them blood, senses, and physical appearance. He gave them the ability to see, hear, touch, taste, and smell. He made them look properly human rather than like animated wood.

The man was named Ask, which meant ash tree. The woman was named Embla, possibly meaning elm. These were the first humans, the ancestors of everyone who would ever live in Midgard.

The gods set Ask and Embla in Midgard and left them to populate the world.

The gods giving life to Ask and Embla.[2]

Humans multiplied and spread across Midgard. They built farms, villages, and eventually the kingdoms that would define the Viking Age. They were always aware that they lived in a world surrounded by danger. Beyond the protective wall of Ymir's eyebrows waited giants, monsters, and chaos. Above them, the gods watched from Asgard. Below them, dwarves crafted wonders in the dark. Around them in the ocean, the World Serpent waited.

The creation of humanity completed the basic structure of the cosmos. All Nine Worlds were now populated. But the cosmos still needed one more element to make it function properly: the passage of time itself, marked by the movement of the sun and moon across the sky.

The sun and moon had been created from the sparks of Muspelheim and placed in chariots that crossed the heavens. But who drove these chariots? The answer involves another family that appears briefly in the myths.

A man named Mundilfari lived in Midgard in those early days. He had two children so beautiful that he couldn't help but boast about them. They were so perfect and radiant that he named them after the celestial bodies themselves: Sól (Sun) and Máni (Moon).

This boasting angered the gods considerably. They didn't appreciate mortals comparing their offspring to celestial phenomena, and they especially didn't appreciate the implication that human children could match the glory of divine creation. So, the gods decided to teach Mundilfari a lesson and make his boast literally true in the most ironic way possible. They took his children from him and set them in the sky to drive the chariots of the sun and moon for all eternity.

Sól drove the sun chariot across the sky each day, bringing light to the worlds. She was accompanied by two horses whose names were Árvakr ("Early Waker") and Alsviðr ("All Swift"), and they pulled her chariot from dawn to dusk without rest. The sun gave off tremendous heat, enough to burn the horses pulling it, so the gods placed bellows called ísarnkol beneath the horses' shoulder blades to cool them as they ran.

Máni drove the moon chariot, marking the passage of nights and months. His horses' names aren't preserved in the sources, but his role was to bring the softer light of the moon to the darkened sky and to mark time's passage through his waxing and waning.

Máni had another task as well. He took two children from Midgard, a boy named Hjúki and a girl named Bil, who had been sent by their father to draw water from the well Byrgir. The children carried the water in a bucket called Sægr using a pole called Simul. Máni took them up into the sky with him, and they can still be seen from Earth. Their shapes are what we see when we look at the face of the moon. The sources do not say whether they wanted to go or were taken by force.

This wasn't a peaceful journey. Two wolves chased the chariots across the sky, born from a giantess in Járnviðr, the "Ironwood." Sköll, whose name means "Treachery" or "Mockery," pursued the sun, running after Sól's chariot from dawn until dusk. Hati Hróðvitnisson ("He Who Hates" or "Enemy of the Gods") chased the moon through the night sky. These wolves were the sons of Fenrir, the great wolf who would one day devour Odin himself.

The wolves would never stop, never rest, and never give up their pursuit. Eclipses happened when the wolves drew close enough that their shadows fell across the sun or moon. People would bang pots and make noise, trying to scare the wolves away. And one day, during Ragnarök, they would catch their prey. Sköll would finally devour the sun. Hati would swallow the moon. The sky would go dark, and the end of everything would begin.

The wolves pursue Sól and Máni.[8]

But that day had not yet come. For now, the sun and moon raced across the heavens, the wolves howled behind them, and time passed in the regular rhythm that allowed life to exist. Days followed nights, seasons turned, years accumulated.

The universe was complete. The stage is set. Now, the real stories—the adventures, betrayals, romances, and disasters that would define Norse mythology—can finally begin.

Chapter 2: The Residents of Asgard

Odin: The All-Father's Obsession

Odin was not a nice god. He was powerful, wise, and respected, but "nice" doesn't appear anywhere in his character description. He was the king of the gods, the All-Father, the one-eyed wanderer who pursued knowledge and power with a single-minded intensity that sometimes horrified even other gods. Understanding Odin means understanding that he operated under the weight of knowing the world's inevitable doom, and that knowledge drove him to actions others found harsh or cruel.

He had more names than any other deity in the Norse pantheon. The sources preserve over two hundred of them. Some

Odin as the wanderer.'

of them include Ygg (The Terrible One), Hár (The High One), Bölverkr (Evil-Doer), Grímnir (The Masked One), and Gangleri (The Wanderer). Each name revealed a different aspect of his nature. He was a shapeshifter, a deceiver, a warrior, a poet, a sorcerer, and a king. He could appear as an old man with a gray beard or a young warrior. He took various forms when it suited his purposes.

Odin's wandering was legendary. He would leave Asgard for extended periods, traveling through all the Nine Worlds in disguise. Sometimes, he appeared as an old man with a staff and a wide-brimmed hat, testing the hospitality of humans or giants. Sometimes, he came as a stranger to halls, challenging people to contests of wisdom and riddles. Those who failed his tests often paid with their lives. Those who succeeded sometimes gained his favor, though Odin's favor was as dangerous as his ire.

He collected knowledge compulsively. Wisdom, prophecy, magic, poetry, runes—Odin wanted to know everything. But knowledge came with a price, and Odin always paid it.

This obsession with knowledge sometimes seemed to exceed even his concern for Asgard's safety. Odin would manipulate humans and gods to learn what he wanted to know. He would betray warriors he'd previously favored if their deaths would serve his purposes. He would break oaths if the knowledge gained outweighed the dishonor of oath-breaking. Other gods found this behavior disturbing, but none dared challenge the All-Father directly.

Odin lived in Asgard in a hall called Valaskjálf, which had a roof made of silver. Inside this hall stood his high seat, Hliðskjálf, from which he could see everything happening in all Nine Worlds. He would sit there and watch, gathering information and observing the movements of gods, giants, elves, dwarves, and humans. Nothing escaped his attention when he sat in that seat.

He had two ravens, Huginn and Muninn, whose names mean "Thought" and "Memory." Every day at dawn, Odin sent these ravens out into the world. They would fly across all the realms, seeing and hearing everything, and at dusk, they would return to perch on Odin's shoulders and whisper what they'd learned into his ears. The poem *Grímnismál*, part of the *Poetic Edda*, records Odin's concern: "I fear for Huginn, that he may not return, but I worry more for Muninn." Odin feared losing Memory more than Thought.

He also had two wolves, Geri and Freki, whose names both meant "greedy" or "ravenous." They sat at his feet during feasts in Valhalla, and Odin would feed them all his food. He himself consumed only wine, something that set him apart from other beings who required sustenance. This wasn't deprivation but rather a sign of how far Odin had transformed himself through his pursuit of wisdom.

His most famous possession was his spear Gungnir, which was forged by the dwarves and said to never miss its target. When Odin threw Gungnir over an army, it meant he was claiming their deaths for himself, marking them for Valhalla, or simply ensuring their doom. He also owned Draupnir, a gold ring that dripped eight new gold rings of equal weight every ninth night, creating endless wealth.

But his most unusual possession was his horse, Sleipnir. This wasn't a normal horse. Sleipnir had eight legs and could travel faster than any other creature in existence. He could gallop across the sky, over the sea, and even journey to Helheim and back. The story of Sleipnir's birth is one of the strangest in Norse mythology, involving Loki transforming into a mare, but we will get to that story later.

A depiction of Sleipnir on a picture stone. [5]

Odin's pursuit of knowledge drove every major decision he made. The most famous example was his sacrifice at Mímir's well. Mímir was a giant of tremendous wisdom who guarded a well beneath one of Yggdrasil's roots. The water in this well contained knowledge and understanding beyond anything else in the Nine Worlds. Odin wanted to drink from it.

But Mímir refused. The price for a single drink, he said, was too high even for the king of the gods.

Odin asked what the price was.

One of Odin's eyes.

Odin didn't hesitate. He plucked out his own eye and dropped it into the well, where it sank to the bottom, staring up through the water forever. Then he drank, and the wisdom he gained from that single drink transformed him. After that, Odin was never depicted with both eyes. He wore a wide-brimmed hat pulled low to hide the missing eye, and he wandered the worlds as a one-eyed old man, trading his depth perception for wisdom.

Later, after a war between the Æsir and Vanir gods, which we'll discuss in the next chapter, Mímir was beheaded by the Vanir, and his head was sent back to Odin. Rather than mourn, Odin preserved Mímir's head with herbs and magic, keeping it alive through enchantments. The head could still speak, so Odin would consult with it when he needed the deepest wisdom. He basically kept this talking severed head as an advisor.

But even sacrificing an eye wasn't enough. Odin wanted more knowledge, specifically the knowledge of runes.

Runes were more than just an alphabet in Norse belief. They were mystical symbols that held power over reality itself. Each rune had a name, a sound, and a meaning that went far beyond simple writing. Knowing the runes meant understanding the fundamental structure of existence, and using them correctly could accomplish anything, from healing to cursing to seeing the future.

The problem was that the runes existed outside the gods' knowledge. They were part of the cosmos itself, hidden and waiting to be discovered by someone willing to pay the price.

Odin paid it.

Hávamál, one of the poems in the *Poetic Edda*, describes what happened in Odin's own words. He hanged himself from Yggdrasil's branches, not as an execution but as a sacrifice—himself to himself. He hung there for nine days and nine nights, wounded by his own spear. He went without food or water, hanging alone and in agony.

The poem says, "I know that I hung on that windy tree, nine long nights, wounded with a spear, dedicated to Odin, myself to myself, on that tree of which no man knows from where its roots run."

Odin was performing the ultimate self-sacrifice, dying without dying, enduring torment to break through to hidden knowledge. On the ninth night, he looked down and saw the runes. He grasped them, screaming, and fell from the tree.

When he rose, he possessed knowledge of the runes. He could use them to heal, harm, protect, curse, see the future, and manipulate fate itself. The price had been nine days of suffering that would have killed any mortal and left even a god transformed.

This sacrifice gave the World Tree its name. Yggdrasil meant "Odin's horse"—the tree he "rode" during his shamanic ordeal.

After gaining knowledge of the runes, Odin taught them to the gods and humans, though he kept the deepest and most powerful rune magic for himself. He became associated with poetry, prophecy, magic, and the dead. He practiced seiðr, a form of magic associated primarily with women and considered *ergi* (unmanly) for men to practice. This brought him criticism from some sources, but Odin pursued knowledge regardless of social conventions.

Seiðr involved going into trances, manipulating fate, and dealing with spirits. In Norse culture, that kind of indirect power was considered women's work, associated with weaving fate, speaking prophecy, and shaping outcomes from the shadows. For a man to practice it meant stepping outside the role of the warrior. That discomfort didn't disappear just because Odin practiced it. But Odin didn't care about social conventions.

This obsession extended to his relationship with the dead. Odin didn't want just any dead warriors in Valhalla. He wanted the best, the most skilled, and the fiercest. His Valkyries chose warriors from the battlefields, and those chosen would fight in Valhalla until Ragnarök, training for the final battle that Odin knew was coming.

Valhalla was one of Odin's halls in Asgard. It was a massive building with 540 doors so wide that 800 warriors could march through each one abreast. The roof was made of shields, the rafters were spears, and chainmail coats covered the benches. It was designed to house an army, and it was decorated with the implements of death.

The Einherjar—Odin's chosen warriors—followed a strict daily routine. Every morning, they would arm themselves and go out to the fields around Valhalla. There, they would fight each other in massive battles, practicing combat skills and testing themselves against worthy opponents. Warriors who'd been enemies in life fought side by side or against each other to train. All personal feuds were set aside to prepare for Ragnarök.

When evening came, all the Einherjar who'd been killed during the day's fighting would be resurrected, their wounds healed and their strength restored. They would return to Valhalla, where they'd feast on the meat of a boar named Sæhrímnir. This boar was killed and cooked every evening and came back to life every morning, providing endless meat for all the warriors. They drank mead that flowed from the udders of a goat named Heiðrún who ate the leaves of Yggdrasil. Like the boar, Heiðrún produced an unlimited supply of milk.

However, Odin's relationship with warriors extended beyond simply collecting them after death. He would grant victory to his chosen warriors during their lives, helping them win battles and earn glory. Then, when he decided their time had come, he would withdraw his favor and allow them to die so he could claim them for Valhalla. This made Odin both the granter of victory and the cause of defeat.

Vikings understood this and accepted it. You couldn't trust Odin to keep you alive, but if you fought bravely and died well, you might earn a place in his hall. The greatest honor a warrior could achieve was to die in battle and be chosen for Valhalla, where they would spend their time until Ragnarök. Then, they would fight alongside history's greatest warriors in one final glorious battle at the end of everything.

And this leads us to the terrible truth that defined Odin's entire existence. He knew how everything would end. He had the gift of prophecy. He knew that Ragnarök was coming, knew that he would die, and knew that the wolf Fenrir would devour him. Everything he did—every sacrifice, every manipulation, every gathering of warriors—was in preparation for a battle he knew he would lose.

This knowledge didn't make him give up. It just made him more determined. He couldn't change fate or escape what the Norns had woven for him, but he could face it with an army at his back and weapons in hand. He could make the end as glorious and terrible as possible.

Odin was not a god who saved people or answered prayers for help in the way Christians pray to God. He was a god who valued glory, wisdom, and poetry over safety or comfort. He helped those who helped themselves, who sought knowledge, and who faced death with courage. He was the god of kings, poets, and warriors but also the god of wanderers, outcasts, and those who sacrificed everything for what they wanted.

The Vikings understood this. When they prayed to Odin, they weren't asking for protection. They were asking for victory, wisdom, and the courage to face whatever fate had in store.

Thor: More Than Just a Hammer

If Odin was the god kings and poets worshiped, Thor was the god everyone else prayed to. He was the most popular deity in the Norse pantheon, the protector of both gods and humans, and the straightforward warrior who preferred hitting problems with his hammer to thinking too hard about them.

Thor was Odin's son, though his mother was Jörð (Earth) rather than Odin's wife Frigg. This made Thor literally half-god, half-Earth, which explained both his tremendous strength and his connection to humanity and the natural world. He was massive, red-bearded, loud, and hot-tempered. Where Odin was cunning and manipulative, Thor was direct and honest. Where Odin wandered in disguise, Thor announced his presence with thunder.

He lived in Asgard in a hall called Bilskirnir, and it is described in the sources as the largest building in existence. It had 540 rooms, enough to house Thor, his family, and any guests who needed shelter. Unlike Odin's silver-roofed hall with its all-seeing throne, Bilskirnir was a place of hospitality and protection, reflecting Thor's nature as a defender rather than a schemer.

Thor was married to Sif, a goddess whose hair was made of gold. The sources tell us little about Sif's personality or role beyond one famous incident where Loki cut off her hair as a prank, forcing him to replace it with actual gold hair crafted by dwarves. She appears in the myths primarily as Thor's wife, bearing him a daughter named Þrúðr (Strength). Thor also had two sons, Magni (Might) and Móði (Courage), who would survive Ragnarök and inherit Mjölnir after their father's death.

Mjölnir was Thor's hammer, which became a symbol of Thor himself. Mjölnir was more than just a weapon. It was a tool of blessing and consecration, used to hallow marriages, births, and funerals. It always hit its target and always returned to Thor's hand after being thrown. The sources describe it as having a short handle due to a flaw in its creation. Loki had interfered with the dwarves while they were forging it, taking the form of a fly and biting the dwarf working the bellows. This caused the handle to be shorter than intended, but it didn't diminish the hammer's power.

The hammer was so heavy that Thor needed special iron gloves called Járngreipr to wield it properly. He also wore a belt called Megingjörð that doubled his already considerable strength. With these items, Thor was unstoppable in combat.

Thor traveled across the worlds in a chariot pulled by two goats, Tanngrisnir and Tanngnjóstr (Tooth-Grinder and Tooth-Gnasher). These weren't ordinary goats. Thor could kill them and eat them for dinner. As long as he kept all the bones intact and wrapped them in the goatskins, the goats would be alive again the next morning, ready to pull his chariot. This gave Thor a renewable food source during his journeys, though one story tells of a human boy who cracked one of the bones to get at the marrow, causing that goat to be permanently lame in one leg.

Thor's primary job was killing giants. He did not kill all giants—he actually had giant friends and even a giant mother—but he went after the giants who threatened Asgard, Midgard, or the cosmic order. He made regular journeys to Jötunheim specifically to hunt down and kill troublesome giants. His hammer became the weapon giants feared more than anything else in existence.

The sources preserve numerous accounts of Thor's battles. He killed Hrungnir, a giant who challenged him to a

Thor fighting giants.[6]

duel using a whetstone as a weapon—a fragment of which became embedded in Thor's skull. He killed Geirröðr, a giant who tried to trap him in his hall without his hammer or strength-enhancing belt. He killed Þrymr after the giant stole Mjölnir and demanded Freyja as ransom. Thor also killed countless unnamed giants who crossed the boundaries between Jötunheim and the realms of the gods and humans.

These weren't always heroic battles. Sometimes, Thor killed giants who were simply in the wrong place at the wrong time or who had the misfortune to anger him in minor ways. His temper made him quick to jump to violence, and his strength made him lethal. But the giants he killed were usually those who threatened harm to Asgard or Midgard, making his violence protective rather than purely destructive.

Thor also dealt with other threats beyond giants. He fought trolls, monsters, and other supernatural creatures that plagued humans or the gods. When farmers found their crops blighted, they called on Thor. When sailors faced impossible storms, they invoked Thor's protection. When villages were threatened by supernatural forces, Thor was the god they wanted on their side.

The thunder that rolled across the sky was Thor riding his chariot across the clouds. Lightning was Mjölnir being thrown. When Vikings heard storms, they knew Thor was out there, fighting and protecting them from forces that would destroy their world. This made Thor deeply personal to the common people in a way Odin never was.

Archaeological evidence suggests Thor enjoyed widespread popularity. More Viking Age artifacts bear symbols of Thor's hammer than any other religious imagery. People wore Mjölnir pendants as protective amulets. Runestones invoked Thor's protection. Even after Christianity began spreading through Scandinavia, many people continued wearing Thor's hammer alongside or instead of the Christian cross. The sheer number of surviving Mjölnir pendants, given the survival rate of artifacts, points to Thor's importance in Norse religious life.

A silver-gilded Mjölnir found in Sweden.[7]

Thor was very different from his father. He was brave, loyal, protective, and had a legendary temper. He was direct and forceful in his approach to problems. When faced with a challenge, Thor's solution usually involved hitting it with Mjölnir until it stopped being a problem. This directness made him predictable and reliable, though it also left him vulnerable to the kind of clever deceptions and manipulations that Odin employed masterfully.

The sources show Thor's temper repeatedly. In Norse mythology, Thor nearly kills Loki several times for various pranks and betrayals, but is only stopped when the other gods intervene. When Thor was tricked or insulted, his response was violence, which often worked out for him but sometimes created new problems.

However, Thor wasn't stupid, despite later portrayals sometimes suggesting otherwise. He was direct and preferred action to planning, but he could think. In several stories, Thor shows cleverness in dealing with dwarves or giants.

Thor's relationship with Loki was complicated. Loki was Odin's blood brother, which made him something like Thor's uncle, though the family relationships among gods were never quite that clear. Thor and Loki went on many adventures together. Sometimes Loki helped Thor; other times, Loki's scheming created problems that Thor had to solve with violence. Thor clearly didn't trust Loki, but he traveled with him anyway, possibly because Odin commanded it or possibly because Thor found Loki's cleverness useful when dealing with situations where a hammer wouldn't work.

One of Thor's most important attributes was his protection of Midgard. The World Serpent, Jörmungandr, encircled the human realm. Thor and Jörmungandr were destined to kill each other at Ragnarök, and they had several encounters before the end times.

The most famous involved Thor going fishing with a giant named Hymir. Thor baited his hook with an ox head and cast it into the deep ocean. Jörmungandr took the bait. Thor hauled on the line with such force that his feet went through the bottom of the boat. He was pulling the World Serpent up from the ocean floor and would have hauled it all the way up and killed it right there. But Hymir, terrified by what he was seeing, cut the fishing line. The serpent sank back into the depths. Thor was so angry that he punched Hymir overboard.

This story shows Thor's nature. He was protective, brave to the point of recklessness, powerful enough to face cosmic threats, and furious when prevented from protecting those he'd sworn to defend.

Thor would die at Ragnarök after killing Jörmungandr. He would slay the serpent but then stagger back nine paces and fall dead, poisoned by the serpent's venom. His sons would survive to inherit his hammer and help rebuild the new world that would emerge after the flames died down. But Thor himself would die doing exactly what he'd always done: protecting Midgard and fighting the forces that threatened the cosmic order.

The Vikings loved him for it. Thor represented everything they valued: strength, loyalty, protection of the community, and the willingness to face any threat, no matter how dangerous. He wasn't perfect. His temper got him into trouble, his preference for violence over diplomacy sometimes made things worse, and his trust in others occasionally backfired. But he was reliable in the way that mattered most. When you needed protection, Thor would be there with his hammer ready.

Loki: The Problem Child

Loki occupied a unique position in Asgard. He was a jötunn by birth, but a member of the Æsir by oath—specifically, through a blood brotherhood with Odin that bound them together in a way that couldn't be broken by Æsir law. This put him in an awkward position. He was neither fully god nor simply a giant. He was also neither wholly trusted nor completely cast out.

The sources do not explain how or why Odin swore this oath of brotherhood with Loki. But the oath existed, and it made Loki's position complicated. He lived among the gods, participated in their councils, joined their adventures, and married a goddess named Sigyn, who bore him two sons, Narfi and Váli.

Loki was a shapeshifter, capable of transforming into animals or other people. He even changed his sex when it suited his purposes. The sources show him becoming a salmon, a fly, a mare, and an old woman, just to name a few. This ability made him useful but also untrustworthy. You could never be completely sure you were talking to Loki or to someone he was impersonating.

His most common nicknames were "Sly One," "Trickster," and "Sky-Traveler." Later sources called him "Lie-Smith," though this appears to be a later Christian influence trying to associate Loki with the devil. The older sources are more ambiguous about Loki's nature. He wasn't evil exactly. He was chaotic, self-interested, and lacked the honor that Norse culture valued above almost everything else.

Loki's pranks ranged from harmless to catastrophic. He tied his testicles to a goat's beard in a tug-of-war to make a giantess laugh. He stole Iðunn's apples, dooming the gods to age and death. He ruined the gods' attempts to make peace with the giants through petty interference and mockery. Some of his tricks helped the gods, as his shapeshifting and quick thinking got them out of dangerous situations. But just as often, his tricks created the dangerous situation in the first place.

What motivated Loki? The sources don't give us clear answers. Perhaps it was boredom. Or maybe he resented being a giant living among gods who barely tolerated him. He might have found chaos more interesting than order. Or maybe he was testing the gods, seeing how far he could push before they pushed back.

Loki's relationship with the gods followed a pattern. He would create a problem through his actions, the gods would threaten him with death or torture, and then he would solve the problem in a way that usually benefited him somehow. This cycle repeated throughout the myths, with the problems and solutions growing progressively worse until finally Loki crossed a line that couldn't be uncrossed.

The first major example of this pattern involved Iðunn's apples. Iðunn was a goddess who kept apples that prevented the gods from aging. As long as they ate her apples regularly, the gods remained young and strong. This made Iðunn incredibly important to Asgard's survival.

One day, Odin, Hœnir, and Loki were traveling together through the wilderness. They killed an ox and tried to roast it over a fire, but the meat would not cook no matter how long they left it over the flames. While they were puzzling over this, an eagle sitting in a tree above them spoke, offering a deal. If they gave him a share of the meat, he would allow it to cook. The gods agreed, and the meat cooked immediately.

However, when the eagle took his share, he took almost all of it, leaving barely anything for the three gods. Loki was furious. He grabbed a pole and struck the eagle, trying to drive it away. But the pole stuck to the eagle's body, and Loki's hands stuck to the pole. The eagle—actually the giant Þjazi in disguise—flew off with Loki dangling helplessly behind him, smashing him against rocks and trees.

Þjazi dragged Loki over mountains and through valleys until Loki screamed for mercy. Þjazi told Loki that he had to lure Iðunn and her apples out of Asgard's protection. Loki agreed.

When Loki returned to Asgard, he told Iðunn that he had found apples in the forest that were even better than hers. She should come see them and bring her own apples for comparison. Iðunn trusted Loki and followed him outside Asgard's walls. Þjazi grabbed her, transformed back into an eagle, and flew off with her to Jötunheim.

Without Iðunn's apples, the gods began aging rapidly, growing old and weak. The gods figured out Loki was responsible and threatened to kill him. But before they could get their hands on him, Loki transformed into a falcon and flew to Jötunheim. He turned Iðunn into a nut and carried her back to Asgard with Þjazi in pursuit (Þjazi had transformed into an eagle again). The gods killed Þjazi just as he reached Asgard's walls, and Iðunn was restored to her normal form with her apples intact.

Loki had caused the crisis and then solved it, which should have taught the gods not to trust him. It did not. This pattern would repeat over and over again.

Loki's most infamous action involved helping dwarves create the gods' greatest treasures, but in the most chaotic way possible. He had cut off Sif's golden hair as a prank, and Thor threatened to break every bone in his body unless he fixed it. Loki went to the dwarves and convinced them to make new hair for Sif out of actual gold that would grow like real hair.

While he was there, he wagered his head with another group of dwarves that they couldn't make three treasures as fine as the ones the first group had made. This sparked a competition, with Loki transforming into a fly and biting the dwarves to sabotage their work. Despite his interference, the dwarves created Gungnir (Odin's spear), Draupnir (Odin's ring), and Mjölnir (Thor's hammer), among other treasures.

Loki lost the bet but argued that the dwarves could take his head but not his neck—classic trickster logic. The dwarves settled for sewing Loki's lips shut instead, though he eventually got them open again.

But Loki's most problematic attribute wasn't his trickery. It was his children.

Loki had a relationship with a giantess named Angrboða, and with her, he had three children who would become important for setting Ragnarök in motion: Fenrir the wolf, Jörmungandr the World Serpent, and Hel, who became queen of the dead. These offspring would play crucial roles in the doom of the gods, but their stories will be told later.

Although the texts don't explicitly say, his children's fates must have contributed to his growing resentment of the gods and their treatment of him. The final straw came with Baldr's death, which we'll also cover in detail later. Loki caused the death of Odin and Frigg's beloved son through trickery and malice, then showed up at Baldr's funeral feast and insulted every god present.

The gods' patience finally ran out. They hunted Loki down and bound him in a cave with a serpent dripping venom on his face. His wife, Sigyn, stayed with him, holding a bowl to catch the venom, but when she had to empty it, venom would fall on Loki, and his convulsions caused earthquakes. He would remain bound there until Ragnarök.

The punishment of Loki.[8]

Loki is perhaps the most complicated figure in Norse mythology. He helped the gods as often as he harmed them. He was clever, funny, and useful when he wanted to be. But he was also selfish, cruel, and ultimately responsible for starting the chain of events that would end with Ragnarök.

Christians tried to make Loki into a devil figure, the enemy of all that was good. The earlier sources are more nuanced. Loki was a product of his nature as a giant living among gods who never fully accepted him, who used him when convenient and punished him when his chaos went too far. He was both a perpetrator and a victim, helpful and harmful, the problem and sometimes the solution.

The Vikings understood this ambiguity. They didn't worship Loki—no evidence exists of Loki having any cult or temples—but they recognized his role in the myths as necessary. Without Loki, there would be no Mjölnir, Gungnir, or Draupnir. Without Loki, many of the gods' greatest treasures wouldn't exist. But without Loki, Baldr would still be alive, and Ragnarök might never have happened.

The Supporting Cast

Many gods beyond the famous three called Asgard home. Each had their own role, their own personality, and their own place in the cosmic order.

Frigg was Odin's wife and queen of the gods. She was associated with marriage, motherhood, and domestic arts, but she was far more than a simple housewife deity. Frigg possessed the gift of prophecy just as Odin did. She knew the fates of many beings across the Nine Worlds, including things Odin himself did not know. The difference was that Frigg kept silent. Where Odin constantly sought more knowledge and used what he learned to manipulate events, Frigg knew things and said almost nothing.

Frigg had her own hall in Asgard called Fensalir (Marsh Halls), and she often sat at a spindle or loom, an activity that may have had deeper significance than simple weaving. The Norns wove fate at the base of Yggdrasil. Perhaps Frigg's weaving connected to fate in ways the sources don't fully explain.

She had her own attendants and handmaidens, including Fulla, who carried Frigg's ashen box and knew all her secrets; Gná, who ran errands across the worlds; and Hlín, who protected those Frigg wished to spare from danger. These goddesses served Frigg specifically, not Odin or the Æsir, suggesting Frigg had her own sphere of influence separate from her husband's.

The sources preserve very few myths centered on Frigg, and those we have often show her as a grieving mother. Her son Baldr was the light of Asgard, beautiful and beloved by all. When Baldr began having dreams of his own death, Frigg traveled through all the Nine Worlds, extracting oaths from every object, plant, animal, and force of nature that they would not harm Baldr. She missed one tiny plant, mistletoe, which seemed too young and harmless to bother with. That oversight would prove fatal, but we'll return to that story later.

Frigg's silence about what she knew makes her one of the most mysterious figures in the pantheon. Did she know Baldr would die and choose not to prevent it? Did she see Ragnarök coming and accept it as inevitable? Could she have changed events if she'd spoken about them, or was she bound by the same fate the Norns had woven for everyone? The sources don't tell us, and Frigg still isn't talking.

Týr was the god of war and justice, though Thor had largely replaced him as the primary war god by the Viking Age. Týr's importance is evident in that Tuesday (Tyr's Day) is named after him, and he appears in older Germanic sources as a supreme sky god before Odin took that role.

Týr represented a specific kind of warfare—the lawful, honorable kind where oaths were kept and rules were followed even when following them meant defeat or death. This made him different from Odin, who would cheat, lie, and manipulate others to achieve victory. Týr was the god you called on for single combat, duels, and battles where honor mattered more than winning.

Týr was brave above all else. When the gods needed someone to place their hand in Fenrir's mouth as a pledge of good faith, only Týr stepped forward. He knew the gods were lying, and he knew that Fenrir would bite down when he realized the binding couldn't be broken. Týr sacrificed his hand anyway because the alternative was letting Fenrir grow until he could destroy them all.

The loss of his hand diminished Týr's role in Asgard. He could still fight and serve as a god of law and justice, but he was no longer the warrior he'd once been. After that, Týr fought one-handed, which limited his effectiveness in combat. However, his sacrifice was remembered as the epitome of courage and honor. He was willing to lose everything for the sake of keeping the cosmic order intact, even when that meant bearing the physical and social consequences of the gods' deception. At Ragnarök, Týr would fight the monstrous hound Garmr. They would kill each other, a fitting end for a god who'd given everything to keep the monsters bound.

Heimdall was the watchman of the gods, guardian of Bifrost, and one of the strangest figures in Norse mythology. He was called the White God. He was said to need less sleep than a bird and had hearing so good that he could hear grass growing and wool growing on sheep. His eyesight was equally sharp; he could see for hundreds of miles in any direction, day or night.

Heimdall constantly stood watch at the Asgard end of Bifrost, watching for any threat approaching the realm of the gods. He lived in a hall called Himinbjörg (Heaven's Castle) located right at the bridge's end, positioned to see anyone attempting to cross. His senses made him the perfect watchman. Nothing could approach Asgard without Heimdall detecting it.

Heimdall's parentage was unusual. The sources call him the son of nine mothers, all of them sisters, possibly representing the nine waves of the sea. How one being could have nine mothers is never explained, but it did make Heimdall different from the other gods. Some scholars suggest this indicates Heimdall was born of the ocean itself, created from the waves that marked the boundary between the ordered world and the chaos beyond.

He owned the horn Gjallarhorn, which he would blow when Ragnarök began. The sound would be heard in all Nine Worlds, calling the gods to their final battle. Heimdall's role at Ragnarök would be to fight Loki. The two of them would kill each other as the world ended. This enmity between Heimdall and Loki appears in several sources, though the reasons for their mutual hatred are never fully explained.

It is suggested that Heimdall was the father of humanity, having disguised himself and traveled among humans to father the different social classes. This story appears primarily in one poem, *Rígsþula*, and may represent a different tradition from the Ask and Embla creation story. In this version, Heimdall, calling himself Ríg, fathered children with three different couples, creating the thrall class, the free farmer class, and the noble class.

Heimdall giving gifts to humans.[9]

Baldr was Odin and Frigg's son. He is described as the most beautiful, wisest, and most beloved of all the gods. Light shone from him. His judgments were always fair and kind. Everyone who met him loved him. He was so good that his death would mark the beginning of the end.

Baldr had a wife, Nanna, and a son, Forseti, who was a god of justice and law. Baldr lived in a hall called Breiðablik (Broad-Gleaming), where nothing impure could exist. He represented the best of what the gods could be.

The sources describe Baldr as having a unique quality among the gods. While others could be petty, vengeful, or cruel, Baldr seemed incapable of such flaws. He never judged harshly, never sought revenge, and never acted out of anger or spite.

His death would devastate Asgard and start the chain of events leading to Ragnarök. We'll cover that story in detail in Chapter 6, but Baldr's primary role in mythology was to be perfect and then die, showing that even he couldn't escape the fate the Norns had woven.

Bragi was the god of poetry and eloquence. He had runes carved on his tongue and was said to be the wisest of the gods in matters of poetry and wordplay. He was married to Iðunn, the goddess who kept the apples of youth. Bragi's main role seemed to be welcoming dead heroes to Valhalla with poems commemorating their deeds.

Iðunn has already been mentioned as the keeper of the apples that prevented the gods from aging. Without her and her apples, the gods would grow old and weak, eventually dying like mortals. This made her one of the most important goddesses, though she appears in relatively few myths beyond the story of her kidnapping.

Njörðr was originally one of the Vanir gods who came to live in Asgard after the war between the Æsir and Vanir. He was associated with the sea, ships, fishing, and wealth. Sailors and fishermen prayed to Njörðr for safe voyages and good catches.

Freyr was Njörðr's son and one of the most important Vanir gods. He was associated with fertility, prosperity, peace, and good harvests. Farmers prayed to Freyr for abundant crops and healthy livestock. He was described as beautiful and powerful, and he ruled over Álfheim, the realm of the light elves.

Freyr owned several magical possessions, including a ship called Skíðblaðnir that could be folded up and put in a pocket when not in use and a boar named Gullinbursti, whose bristles glowed in the dark. But his most important possession was his sword, which could fight by itself.

Freyr made a terrible mistake that would cost him his life at Ragnarök. He glimpsed a beautiful giant woman named Gerðr and fell desperately in love. He sent his servant Skírnir to woo her on his behalf, but Skírnir demanded Freyr's sword as payment. Freyr gave it to him, trading his greatest weapon for a wife. This meant that at Ragnarök, when Freyr faced the fire giant Surtr, he would be without his sword.

Freyja was Freyr's twin sister and possibly the most powerful of all the goddesses. She was associated with love, beauty, fertility, war, and death—an unusual combination that made her both desirable and dangerous. She was so beautiful that gods and giants constantly tried to win her hand, and her necklace, Brísingamen, was said to be the most beautiful object in existence.

The story of how Freyja acquired Brísingamen reveals her willingness to do whatever it took to get what she wanted. She saw four dwarves crafting a golden necklace of surpassing beauty and demanded to buy it. The dwarves refused gold or any conventional payment. They would give her the necklace only if she spent a night with each of them. Freyja agreed without hesitation. She spent four nights in the dwarves' underground hall and emerged with Brísingamen, which she wore from that moment forward.

Freyja was also a warrior goddess. She got first choice of the slain in battle, taking half of them to her hall, Fólkvangr. This division of the dead suggests Freyja's power rivaled Odin's, at least in some spheres. What happened to the warriors Freyja chose? The sources don't tell us much about Fólkvangr or what the dead did there, but they suggest an afterlife separate from Valhalla's eternal training for Ragnarök.

Freyja practiced seiðr magic and taught it to Odin. That Odin learned seiðr from her suggests she possessed knowledge even the All-Father lacked. She could transform into a bird using a cloak of falcon feathers. She rode a chariot pulled by cats. She owned a boar named Hildisvíni that she sometimes rode into battle. She was fierce, independent, and willing to use any means necessary to get what she wanted.

The sources preserve several stories of giants trying to obtain Freyja as a wife, and in each case, the gods go to extreme lengths to prevent it. When the builder who constructed Asgard's wall demanded Freyja as payment, the gods panicked. When the giant Þrymr stole Thor's hammer, he demanded Freyja as ransom. Thor had to dress as Freyja and infiltrate the giant's hall to get Mjölnir back.

Why were the gods so protective of Freyja? Partly because losing her to the giants would mean losing her beauty and magic, but it was also because Freyja had no intention of being traded to giants like a piece of property. She was desired but never owned. She chose her own lovers, made her own decisions, and answered to no one. The gods protected Freyja because she demanded protection and because the alternative was facing her fury. The sources don't tell us what happened to her at Ragnarök, which may mean she survived. However, it also may mean that her fate wasn't considered important enough to record.

The Valkyries: Odin's Choosers of the Slain

The Valkyries were supernatural beings who served Odin and dwelt in Asgard. Their exact nature varied across sources. Sometimes they were treated as minor deities or *dísir* (guardian spirits). Sometimes they were depicted as elevated mortal women and other times as purely supernatural creatures. What remained the same was their job. They were to select warriors from battlefields and bring them to Valhalla. Their name meant "choosers of the slain," and they appeared on battlefields as beautiful women in armor or sometimes as ravens or wolves.

The Valkyries determined who won and who lost in battle. When they decided a warrior's time had come, they would mark him for death and then carry his spirit to Valhalla while his body fell on the battlefield. This made them both terrifying and honored. Warriors wanted to be chosen by the Valkyries because it meant entrance to Valhalla, but it also meant dying in battle rather than living to old age.

The sources describe the Valkyries' appearance in different ways. Sometimes they were beautiful women on horseback, riding through the air above battlefields. Sometimes they appeared as ravens or wolves, circling above the fallen. Sometimes they were simply a feeling, a knowledge that your death had arrived and the choosers were watching. Warriors who claimed to have seen Valkyries described them as tall, fierce, and terrifyingly beautiful, with armor that shone like ice and eyes that saw through to your worthiness.

Different sources give different names and numbers of Valkyries. Some list thirteen, some nine, some fewer. The names we have include Brynhildr (Armor-Battle), Göndul (Wand-Wielder), Geirskögul (Spear-Skögul), Hildr (Battle), Mist (Cloud), Ráðgríðr (Plan-Destroyer), Reginleif (Heritage of the Gods), Skögul (Shaker), and Þrúðr (Strength, also mentioned as Thor's daughter in some sources). Each name suggested combat, fate, or choosing, reflecting their function.

The Valkyries served Odin, but they weren't mindless servants. Several stories show Valkyries making their own choices, falling in love with mortal warriors, or defying Odin's commands and facing punishment for it. The most famous Valkyrie is Brynhildr, whose story is told in the *Volsunga Saga*.

Brynhildr disobeyed Odin by granting victory to the wrong warrior in a battle. The sources do not explain her reasoning. She may have loved the warrior Odin had marked for death, disagreed with Odin's judgment, or was testing her own authority against his. What matters is that she made a choice that contradicted Odin's will.

Odin's punishment was severe. He pricked her with a sleep-thorn and placed her in an enchanted sleep on a mountaintop, surrounded by a wall of fire. She would remain there, neither fully alive nor dead, until a hero brave enough to cross the flames came to wake her. Odin decreed that whoever woke her would marry her, binding her fate to a mortal hero rather than allowing her to continue as a Valkyrie.

The hero who eventually crossed the flames was Sigurd, one of the greatest warriors in Norse legend. Sigurd was the son of Sigmund, descended from Volsung, and raised by a smith named Regin. Regin taught Sigurd smithcraft, but Regin had his own agenda. Regin's brother, Fafnir, had killed their father, Hreidmar, to claim a hoard of cursed gold and then transformed into a dragon to guard it. Regin wanted Sigurd to kill Fafnir, so Regin could claim the treasure. He reforged the shards of Sigurd's father's broken sword into a blade called Gram, which was powerful enough to kill a dragon.

Sigurd killed Fafnir by digging a pit in the dragon's path and stabbing upward into its belly as it crawled over. As Fafnir died, he warned Sigurd that the gold was cursed and would bring death to whoever possessed it. Sigurd took the treasure anyway.

While roasting Fafnir's heart for Regin, Sigurd burned his finger on the hot meat and put it in his mouth to cool it. Fafnir's blood gave him the ability to understand the speech of birds. He heard birds discussing how Regin planned to kill him and take the treasure for himself. So, Sigurd killed Regin before Regin could betray him.

Now Sigurd had the cursed treasure, a powerful sword, and the ability to understand bird speech. The birds told him about a woman sleeping on a mountain, surrounded by fire, more beautiful than any other. Sigurd rode to find her.

When he reached the mountain, he saw the wall of flames encircling the peak. Without hesitation, he rode his horse Grani straight through the fire. The flames didn't harm him—whether because of his courage, his fate, or some protection from the cursed treasure, the sources don't specify clearly.

On the mountaintop, he found a figure in full armor, sleeping. When he cut away the armor, he discovered it was a woman. It was Brynhildr. She woke and immediately knew what had happened. She had been waiting for the hero brave enough to cross the flames, and Sigurd was that hero.

Brynhildr taught Sigurd wisdom and runes, sharing the knowledge a Valkyrie possessed. They fell in love and pledged to marry. Sigurd gave her a ring from Fafnir's treasure. This ring would later cause tremendous suffering, as the treasure was cursed.

But for the time being, Sigurd rode away from the mountain, planning to return after completing other deeds. He came to the court of King Gjuki, whose wife Grimhild was skilled in magic and manipulation. Grimhild wanted Sigurd to marry her daughter Gudrun, binding this great warrior to their family. She gave Sigurd a potion that made him forget

Brynhildr entirely. Under the potion's influence, Sigurd married Gudrun, believing he had never loved anyone else.

Grimhild then convinced Sigurd to help her son Gunnar win Brynhildr as a bride. Gunnar rode to the mountain with the wall of fire, but his horse refused to cross the flames. Gunnar's horse wouldn't enter the fire, and Gunnar himself lacked the courage to cross alone.

So, Sigurd and Gunnar used magic to exchange shapes. In Gunnar's form, Sigurd rode through the flames again on Grani and found Brynhildr. She had been waiting years for Sigurd to return and marry her as he had promised. When he never came back, she believed he'd abandoned her. Now here was another hero crossing the flames, proving the prophecy could be fulfilled by someone else. In her anger at Sigurd's betrayal and bound by Odin's decree that she would marry whoever crossed the flames, she accepted this new hero as her husband. She didn't recognize that the man in Gunnar's shape was actually Sigurd himself, enchanted and unable to remember her. He stayed three nights with her but placed his sword, Gram, between them in the bed, maintaining the deception.

They returned, and Brynhildr married Gunnar. She had given up on her first love and accepted this new fate, not knowing the terrible truth.

One day, the queens—Brynhildr and Gudrun—quarreled about whose husband was greater. In anger, Gudrun revealed that Sigurd had crossed the flames for Brynhildr, not Gunnar. She showed Brynhildr the ring Sigurd had taken from her during that deceptive visit. It was the same ring Sigurd had originally given Brynhildr as a pledge of their love.

Brynhildr realized she had been betrayed. The hero who'd woken her, whom she'd loved and taught, had forgotten her through magic and helped another man trick her into marriage. She had married the wrong man. Her true love had married her husband's sister.

Brynhildr's rage and grief were absolute. She convinced Gunnar and his brothers to kill Sigurd, claiming he had dishonored her. The curse on Fafnir's treasure was working its way through everyone who touched it, turning love to hatred and loyalty to murder.

Gunnar's brother Guttorm killed Sigurd in his bed. As Sigurd died, he killed Guttorm in return. Brynhildr heard Sigurd's death cry and knew her revenge was complete.

But revenge brought no satisfaction. Brynhildr realized that she had destroyed the man she loved and that she had been manipulated by Grimhild's magic just as Sigurd had been. She announced that she would follow Sigurd to death. Despite everyone's attempts to stop her, she stabbed herself with a sword.

Before dying, Brynhildr prophesied the future sorrows that would come from the cursed treasure—how Gudrun would suffer, how Gunnar would die, and how the gold would continue spreading death. Then she died.

They burned Sigurd and Brynhildr together on the same funeral pyre. In death, they were reunited as they should have been in life, before magic, deception, and cursed gold destroyed everything.

This story shows that even Valkyries were subject to Odin's will and to fate's decrees. Brynhildr had the power to decide who lived and died in battle, but she couldn't escape the consequences of defying Odin, and she couldn't escape the doom woven by the Norns.

In Valhalla, the Valkyries served mead to the Einherjar, the dead warriors who trained there for Ragnarök. They would bring horns of mead to the warriors during the nightly feasts, and in the morning, they would watch the warriors fight, die, and resurrect again, practicing for the final battle. This dual role—choosers of the slain on battlefields and servants in Valhalla—made Valkyries essential to Odin's preparations for Ragnarök.

Archaeological evidence shows that the Vikings took Valkyries seriously. Grave goods in high-status female burials sometimes include weapons and armor, possibly indicating women who served as priestesses of Freyja or who were buried with the accessories of Valkyries. Amulets depicting armed women on horseback have been found throughout Scandinavia. Picture stones from Gotland show female figures carrying drinking horns, interpreted as Valkyries welcoming dead warriors to the afterlife.

A picture stone of a Valkyrie welcoming a man with a horn of mead.[10]

The sources don't specify what would happen to the Valkyries at Ragnarök. Would they fight alongside the Einherjar they'd chosen? Would they continue serving Odin until he fell to Fenrir? Would they survive to serve whatever came after? The myths are silent on this point, leaving the Valkyries' ultimate fate as mysterious as their origins. Perhaps they would fall with the gods they served, or perhaps they would live to choose the slain in whatever battles came after the world's rebirth.

Chapter 3: Love, War, and Magic

The Aesir-Vanir War

The gods were not always united. Before the cosmic order we've been discussing settled into place, two tribes of gods existed separately: the Æsir and the Vanir. The Æsir, led by Odin, were generally associated with warfare, sovereignty, and order—the structured power of kings and warriors. The Vanir were generally associated with fertility, prosperity, and the natural world—the cyclical power of seasons, crops, and abundance. But these weren't absolute categories. Odin was a master of magic, something that was typically associated with the Vanir. Freyr, though a Vanir god, became a patron of kings and warriors. These two groups went to war, and that war shaped the divine politics of the Nine Worlds.

The sources don't give us a clear, detailed account of how the war started or how long it lasted. What we have are fragments and allusions scattered across different texts. The *Völuspá* mentions it briefly in a few stanzas. Snorri's *Prose Edda* provides some details but leaves many questions unanswered. What emerges from these fragments is a conflict neither side could win and a resolution that involved merging the two groups rather than keeping them separate.

The war began, according to the most common version, with a mysterious figure named Gullveig. Her name means "Gold-Drink" or "Gold-Power." She appeared in Asgard one day. The sources describe her as skilled in magic, particularly seiðr. She may have been a Vanir goddess, a *völva* (a seeress) testing the Æsir, or something else entirely.

The Æsir didn't trust her. They may have feared her power, or perhaps they didn't like what she represented. The *Völuspá* says she came to the gods, prophesying in trances and practicing seiðr.

The Æsir tried to kill her. They stabbed her with spears and threw her body into a fire in Odin's hall. But Gullveig didn't stay dead. She emerged from the flames alive, possibly even more powerful than before. The Æsir burned her again. She survived again. Three times they tried to destroy her by burning, and three times she returned. After the third burning, she took the name Heiðr ("Bright One" or "Honor") and traveled the world practicing seiðr.

This attempted murder violated fundamental laws. Although the sources don't say explicitly, her attempted execution appears to have been the catalyst for conflict. The Vanir demanded compensation. The Æsir refused or perhaps gave an inadequate response. War followed.

The conflict was brutal. The sources describe the walls of Asgard being breached, which suggests the Vanir were powerful enough to threaten the Æsir's home directly. The *Völuspá* mentions that the Vanir "trod the fields" and broke down walls. Both sides had skilled warriors and powerful magic.

Neither side could achieve a decisive victory. The war dragged on, devastating both groups without resolving anything. Eventually, both sides realized that continuing the conflict served no purpose. They called a truce and negotiated terms.

The peace agreement involved an exchange of hostages. High-ranking members of each group would go live with the other side as guarantees of good behavior. The Vanir sent Njörðr and his children, Freyr and Freyja, to live in Asgard. The Æsir sent Hœnir and Mimir to live with the Vanir.

This exchange worked out better for one side than the other.

Njörðr, Freyr, and Freyja integrated smoothly into Asgard. Njörðr became associated with the sea and wealth. Freyr took charge of rain, sunshine, and prosperity. Freyja brought her powerful seiðr magic and taught it to Odin himself. All three became essential members of the Æsir, and they were respected and honored. Freyr and Freyja were so important that they were worshiped alongside Odin and Thor in many temples.

The Æsir hostages didn't fare as well. Hœnir appeared impressive. He was tall, handsome, and looked every bit the leader. But according to Snorri's account in the *Ynglinga Saga*, he had a problem. He couldn't make decisions on his own. Whenever the Vanir asked Hœnir for advice or judgment, he would say, "Let others decide." If Mimir wasn't there to whisper answers, Hœnir was useless.

The Vanir felt cheated. They'd sent three of their best gods to Asgard and received one impressive-looking fool and one genuinely wise advisor in return. They couldn't kill Hœnir without breaking the peace, but they could express their displeasure. They beheaded Mimir, who was seen as just an advisor, and sent his head back to Odin.

Odin's response to receiving his advisor's severed head was characteristically pragmatic. He preserved Mimir's head with herbs and incantations, keeping it alive so it could speak. The head retained all of Mimir's wisdom, and Odin would consult with it when he needed counsel. The Vanir had meant to insult Odin by killing Mimir, but instead, they'd given him a permanent advisor who would never die or betray him.

The war ended with an unusual ceremony that sealed the peace. Both groups of gods gathered, and each one spat into a large vessel. This wasn't a crude gesture but a ritual act with deep significance. Spittle contained something of the person's essence—their breath and life force. By combining their spit, the Æsir and Vanir were literally mixing their essences together.

From the combined spit of all the gods, they created a being named Kvasir. He was the wisest being ever to exist, containing the combined wisdom of both divine tribes. Kvasir could answer any question put to him. There was no mystery he couldn't solve, no problem he couldn't address, and no question that could stump him. Kvasir traveled the worlds, and the sources tell us he shared his knowledge with those who asked.

Things didn't end well for Kvasir. Two dwarves, Fjalar and Galar, invited him to a private feast. These dwarves were not honorable craftsmen but murderers who saw an opportunity. When Kvasir arrived, they killed him. They drained his blood into three containers, two vats called Són and Boðn, and a pot called Óðrerir. They mixed his blood with honey, and this mixture became the Mead of Poetry.

Anyone who drank this mead would become a skilled poet or scholar, able to speak with wisdom and compose beautiful verses. The dwarves had transformed Kvasir's wisdom into a consumable form, but it came at the cost of murdering the being who'd embodied peace between the gods.

The war transformed the divine order. After the exchange of hostages, the distinction between Æsir and Vanir became less important. Some Vanir gods even came to live and rule alongside the Æsir in Asgard, working together to maintain cosmic order and facing threats together. The two tribes hadn't exactly merged, though, as the Vanir gods retained their distinct characteristics and powers.

This shows that even among gods, conflict could end in integration rather than total victory. Freyja's magic strengthened the Æsir, while Odin's strategic thinking helped the Vanir find their place. The cosmic order benefited from both tribes working together.

Njord and Skadi: When Opposites Don't Attract

Njörðr came to Asgard as a hostage after the war, but he became a respected god of the sea, sailing, fishing, and wealth. He lived at Nóatún (Ship-Enclosure), a hall by the sea where he could watch the waves and ships. Sailors prayed to Njörðr for safe voyages and good catches. His association with wealth made him popular among merchants and anyone who made their living from the sea.

Njörðr's marriage to the giantess Skaði is one of the stranger stories in Norse mythology, and it reveals something important about how the gods handled obligations and how some compromises simply don't work, no matter how hard you try.

The story begins with Skaði's father, a giant named Þjazi. Þjazi was the one who'd kidnapped Iðunn and her youth-giving apples after Loki lured her out of Asgard's protection. When Loki brought Iðunn back, Þjazi pursued them in eagle form. The gods killed Þjazi as he reached Asgard's walls, ending the threat but creating a new problem.

Skaði arrived at Asgard fully armed and ready for vengeance. She was a formidable warrior, skilled with the bow, and she lived in the mountains where she hunted and skied. Her father's death demanded compensation according to Norse custom, and she had the strength to enforce her demands.

The gods didn't want another war. They'd just finished fighting the Vanir, and Skaði was dangerous enough on her own without risking other giants joining her cause. So, they negotiated. Odin made the first gesture by taking Þjazi's eyes and throwing them into the sky, where they became stars. This gave Þjazi a kind of immortality, with his eyes watching over the world forever.

But Skaði wanted more than memorial stars. She demanded two things. First, the gods had to make her laugh, something she declared impossible given her grief. Second, she wanted to choose a husband from among the gods.

The gods agreed to both conditions, but they added a catch to the second one. Skaði could choose her husband, but she could only see the gods' feet. Nothing else.

Why feet? The sources don't explain the gods' reasoning. Perhaps they wanted to make the choice more random, preventing Skaði from simply choosing the most powerful or attractive god and creating political complications. Perhaps they thought this limitation was fair compensation that still gave Skaði agency. She got to choose, but under constraints that protected the gods' interests. Or perhaps they were testing whether Skaði would accept terms that seemed designed to frustrate her.

Skaði accepted the terms. She was practical and understood that, as one giantess facing all the gods of Asgard, she wasn't in a position to demand better conditions. She'd gotten them to agree to choose a husband from their ranks, which was more than many would have expected.

The gods lined up behind a curtain or screen, showing only their feet. Skaði walked along the line, examining each pair carefully. She was looking for beauty, for perfection, for feet that would indicate the god she wanted.

She saw weathered feet, callused from travel and battle. She saw strong feet, thick and powerful. She saw feet that told stories of their owners' lives and activities. And then she saw one pair that stood out. They were perfectly formed feet, clean and beautiful, unblemished and graceful.

Skaði was certain these belonged to Baldr. Baldr was the most beautiful of all the gods, beloved and perfect in every way. Of course, his feet would be the most beautiful too. She made her choice, pointing to these feet and declaring she would marry whoever owned them.

The curtain was pulled back. The feet belonged to Njörðr.

Njörðr's feet were beautiful because he spent his life by the sea, walking on smooth sand and wading in clean water. The ocean had washed and smoothed his feet until they were flawless. Baldr, for all his beauty, didn't have the same advantage.

Skaði had picked the sea god when she wanted the god of light. But she'd made her choice according to the rules they'd agreed on, and Norse culture took such agreements seriously. Skaði married Njörðr.

Before the wedding, the gods still had to fulfill the first part of her demands. They had to make her laugh. This is where Loki comes in. He tied one end of a rope to a goat's beard and the other end to his own testicles. The goat pulled one way, and Loki pulled the other, both shrieking in pain. Loki eventually fell into Skaði's lap. She couldn't help but laugh.

Skaði and Njörðr tried to make their marriage work. They eventually agreed on a compromise. They would spend nine nights at Skaði's home in the mountains (Þrymheimr) and nine nights at Njörðr's home by the sea (Nóatún). This seemed fair, but it failed.

After nine nights in the mountains, Njörðr couldn't stand it anymore. He hated the mountains, he said. The howling of wolves sounded ugly to him compared to the song of swans.

Skaði had her own complaints after nine nights by the sea. She couldn't sleep for the crying of birds. The gulls woke her each morning when they came from the ocean.

Njörðr needed the sea. Skaði needed the mountains. Neither could bear the other's home.

They tried, but some compromises don't work. Njörðr and Skaði separated, each returning to their preferred realm. Skaði went back to the mountains, where she hunted with her bow and skied across the slopes. Njörðr returned to his hall by the sea.

The marriage wasn't annulled. That wasn't really an option in Norse culture, and besides, the union had been part of the compensation for Þjazi's death. But they lived separately, acknowledging that forcing two fundamentally incompatible people to share a life did no one any good.

Some later sources suggest Skaði eventually married someone more suited to her nature, possibly even Odin, who was fond of wandering mountains in disguise, but these traditions are less certain.

This story is about the clash between the sea and the mountains, two forces that cannot coexist. Njörðr and Skaði weren't bad people. They weren't cruel to each other. They genuinely tried to make things work. But their natures were opposed.

Freyr's Sacrifice for Love

Freyr made a terrible mistake, and it started with sitting in a place he had no business sitting.

Odin's high seat, Hliðskjálf, allowed whoever sat in it to see everything happening in all the Nine Worlds. This was Odin's privilege, part of his role as All-Father and his endless quest for knowledge. But one day, when Odin was away, Freyr decided to sit in the high seat and look out across the worlds.

He gazed across the realms, seeing mountains and seas, forests and halls, and gods, giants, and humans going about their lives. And then he looked toward Jötunheim, the land of the giants, and saw something that changed everything.

A woman was walking toward a hall. As she lifted her arms to open the door, light shone from her arms and hands so brightly that it illuminated the sky and sea. She was extraordinarily beautiful, and the light that came from her was like nothing Freyr had ever seen.

Her name was Gerðr, and she was a giant's daughter.

Freyr was smitten instantly. *Skírnismál*, the poem that tells this story, describes him becoming lovesick to the point of illness. He stopped eating. He stopped sleeping. He stopped speaking to anyone. He just sat alone, consumed by desire for Gerðr, growing weaker and more miserable every day.

Freyr's father, Njörðr, noticed his son's condition and sent Freyr's servant Skírnir to find out what was wrong. Skírnir was Freyr's most trusted servant. He was brave and clever, the kind of person you could rely on for dangerous or delicate tasks. When Skírnir asked what was troubling him, Freyr finally confessed. He had seen Gerðr and fallen in love with her. He was dying from wanting someone he could never have.

But why couldn't he have her? Well, Gerðr was a giant's daughter, and the relationship between gods and giants was complicated. Some gods married giants. Njörðr had married Skaði, after all, though that hadn't worked out. But courtship between gods and giants was always fraught with danger, politics, and the very real possibility that the giant's family would try to kill the suitor.

Freyr couldn't court Gerðr himself. As one of the major Vanir gods, he had responsibilities in Asgard. He was also apparently too lovesick to function. So, he asked Skírnir to go to Jötunheim and woo Gerðr on his behalf.

Skírnir agreed, but he set conditions. He demanded Freyr's sword as payment for this task. This was not just any sword. Freyr's sword was one of the most powerful weapons in existence. It could fight by itself, needing no hand to guide it. In battle, Freyr could simply set the sword loose, and it would cut down his enemies without him needing to swing it.

This was an enormous price. Freyr's sword was his primary defense, the weapon that made him formidable in combat. Without it, he would be vulnerable at Ragnarök when he faced Surtr and the fire giants. The prophecies were clear. Freyr would die fighting Surtr, and losing his sword would make that death certain.

Freyr knew all this. He still gave Skírnir the sword anyway. Freyr was willing to trade his life, or at least his chance of surviving Ragnarök, for the possibility of marrying Gerðr. Love mattered more to him than survival. The woman who shone with light meant more than his own life.

Skírnir took the sword and rode to Jötunheim. The journey was dangerous from the start. He had to cross through walls of flame to reach Gerðr's father's hall, a test that would have killed any normal being. Skírnir had Freyr's magical sword, but he also had courage and determination.

When he arrived at Gerðr's father's hall, enormous dogs guarded the entrance. These fierce hounds would tear apart any intruder. A shepherd sat nearby, watching both the hounds and the strange sight of a god's servant arriving at a giant's hall. Skírnir spoke to the shepherd, asking how he might approach Gerðr without being killed by the dogs or her father.

The shepherd's response was grim. There was no safe way. Gerðr's father would kill any god's servant who tried to approach his daughter. The dogs would attack. Skírnir would die before he ever reached her.

But Skírnir had come too far to turn back. He used magic and threats to get past the obstacles, finally reaching Gerðr herself. When she saw him, she was not impressed. A god's servant had come to her father's hall uninvited, demanding she agree to marry someone she'd never met. This was not romantic. This was presumptuous and potentially dangerous for her and her family.

Skírnir offered her treasures first. Eleven golden apples, not Iðunn's apples of youth, but valuable nonetheless. Gerðr refused them. "I will not accept the eleven apples for any man," she said. She and Freyr would never live together as long as they both lived, she declared. She lived comfortably in her father's hall, wanted for nothing, and saw no reason to trade that security for marriage to a stranger.

Skírnir then offered her Draupnir, Odin's ring that dripped eight new gold rings every ninth night. This was an incredible gift, as it guaranteed eternal wealth. Even Odin valued the ring. Gerðr refused that too. She had no need of wealth or treasures, no matter how magical or valuable.

When gifts failed, Skírnir tried threats. He drew Freyr's sword and threatened to cut off her head if she didn't agree to the marriage. Gerðr wasn't impressed. She said her father, Gymir, would fight Skírnir if he tried to harm her, and besides, she wasn't the kind of woman who could be threatened into marriage. "I think I know you. You don't have the courage to fight against Gymir."

Finally, Skírnir turned to magic. He took up his staff and began to carve runes while speaking a curse so detailed and horrific that it fills several stanzas of *Skírnismál*. This wasn't a simple threat. This was binding magic that would absolutely ruin Gerðr's existence if she continued refusing.

Skírnir would carve *þurs* (giant), *nauð* (need, distress), and other runes on Gerðr. He would strike her with his staff and tame her to his will. She would go where she would never again be seen by humans. She would sit on an eagle's perch at the edge of the world, looking outward at Helheim. Food would be disgusting to her. She would become a spectacle and be more famous than the watchman of the gods. She would be consumed by a desire that could never be satisfied. She would be like a thistle pressed down in a harvest barn, withered, useless, and destroyed.

However, Skírnir could smooth away the curse if she accepted. But if she refused, these runes would remain carved forever.

This curse was terrifying. It didn't just threaten death. That would have been merciful. It threatened eternal isolation, unfulfilled longing, wasting away without dying, and being conscious and aware but unable to find any comfort or satisfaction.

This finally convinced her. She agreed to meet Freyr, though she made him wait nine nights before she would come. *Skírnismál* presents this as Gerðr's consent, but the poem doesn't explicitly judge whether this represents coercion, inevitable fate, or perhaps a ritualized courtship test that had to be passed. How the original audiences understood this moment, as love magic, as force, or as something else, remains ambiguous in the sources.

Freyr was impatient. Just one night would feel long, but he had to endure nine? But the nine nights passed, and Gerðr came to meet Freyr. They married, and according to the sources, the marriage was successful. Unlike Njörðr and Skaði, Freyr and Gerðr were compatible. They loved each other, or at least the sources don't record any complaints from either of them.

Different readers interpret this story differently. Some see it as foolish. Freyr doomed the world for a woman he'd glimpsed once from Odin's throne. Others see it as heroic. Freyr chose love over fear, choosing to live fully rather than simply prepare for death.

The Magic of the North

Magic in Norse belief wasn't a single unified system. Different types of magic existed, each with its own practices, purposes, and social implications. Understanding these distinctions helps explain why Odin practiced magic that was considered shameful for men, why Freyja was feared as well as loved, and why prophecy was both respected and terrifying.

Seiðr was the most powerful and most controversial form of magic. It involved going into trances, communicating with spirits, and manipulating fate itself. Practitioners of seiðr could see the future, curse enemies, heal or harm others, and influence events that hadn't happened yet. This wasn't subtle magic. Seiðr practitioners (seiðkona if female, seiðmaðr if male) would sit on a high platform and enter trance states.

The practice had specific procedures and tools. A seiðr ceremony typically involved building a special platform or using a designated high seat called a seiðhjallr. The practitioner would sit there while assistants or participants formed a circle around them. The assistants would sing songs called varðlokur (ward songs or guardian songs), creating the environment that allowed the seiðkona or seiðmaðr to enter trance.

Once in trance, the practitioner's spirit could leave their body and travel to other realms. They might visit the world of the dead to speak with spirits who had knowledge of the future. They might journey to the realm of the giants to discover hidden information. Their body would remain on the platform, sometimes appearing dead or deeply asleep, while their consciousness wandered.

Seiðr was considered *ergi* (unmanly or effeminate) for men to practice. This gendered stigma was likely related to how seiðr involved a kind of passive receptivity, allowing spirits to enter a person and letting themselves be penetrated by supernatural forces. Men were expected to be active and dominant, not receptive and passive. The practice also involved a loss of control that may have contradicted masculine ideals of self-mastery.

This made Odin's practice of seiðr scandalous. The king of the gods engaged in magic that his culture considered shameful for men. Some sources suggest he was criticized for this. But Odin didn't care about social conventions when knowledge was at stake. He wanted the knowledge and power seiðr provided, and he was willing to cross social boundaries to get it.

Freyja was the greatest practitioner of seiðr. The sources tell us that Freyja was the first to bring seiðr to the Æsir, suggesting it originated with the Vanir or perhaps with the giants. Under Freyja's instruction, Odin learned to enter trance states, speak with the dead, and see possible futures.

One famous account of a seiðr ceremony appears in the *Saga of Erik the Red*. A seeress named Þorbjörg arrives at a farm during a famine. The household prepares for her visit by building a high platform and preparing specific foods. Þorbjörg wears elaborate clothing, including a cloak of black lambskin lined with white catskin, calfskin shoes, and catskin gloves. She carries a staff decorated with brass and set with stones. She eats a special meal made from the hearts of all available animals.

The ceremony itself requires women who know the ward songs. A woman named Guðríðr reluctantly agrees to sing, explaining that she learned the songs from her foster mother but is now Christian and shouldn't participate in pagan practices. She sings anyway, and Þorbjörg enters her trance, communicates with spirits, and returns with prophecies about when the famine will end and what will happen to various members of the community.

This account, while written down by Christians and possibly colored by Christian perspectives, gives us one of the few detailed descriptions of how seiðr ceremonies actually worked.

Galdr was different from seiðr in almost every way. This was magic based on chanting and runes, making it more active and direct than seiðr's trances. Galdr involved speaking or singing words of power, often incorporating runes into the chants. The Old Norse word *galdr* comes from a root meaning "to crow" or "to chant," and the practice involved sustained vocalization of magical formulas.

Men could practice galdr without social stigma. It was considered a more masculine form of magic, as it was direct and forceful. A person had to use their voice and will to impose change on the world rather than opening themselves to spirits. Warriors might chant a galdr before battle to strengthen their weapons or protect themselves. Rune masters used galdr when carving runes to activate their power.

The runes themselves were central to galdr magic. Each rune had a name, a sound, and layers of meaning that went far beyond simple writing. Learning the runes meant understanding not just how to write them but also what they meant, how they connected to cosmic forces, and how to use them to accomplish specific goals.

The Elder Futhark, the oldest runic alphabet, contained twenty-four runes divided into three groups of eight called *ætts* (families). Each rune had its own power and significance.

Fehu (ᚠ) meant cattle or wealth, representing prosperity and abundance.

Uruz (ᚢ) meant aurochs (wild ox), symbolizing strength and primal power.

Þurisaz (ᚦ) meant giant or thorn, used for both attack and defense.

Ansuz (ᚨ) meant god or mouth, connected to communication and divine power.

Raidho (ᚱ) meant wagon or journey, representing travel and the right path.

Kenaz (ᚲ) meant torch, symbolizing knowledge and illumination.

Gebo (ᚷ) meant gift, representing exchange and hospitality.

Wunjo (ᚹ) meant joy or harmony.

Each rune could be used alone or in combination with others. A skilled rune master could weave together multiple runes to create complex magical effects.

Odin gained understanding of the runes through his nine-day ordeal on Yggdrasil. After that sacrifice, he could use runes for healing, binding, cursing, protecting, and seeing hidden things. The *Hávamál* lists eighteen rune spells Odin knows, including spells to calm strife, dull an enemy's weapons, break chains, deflect arrows, extinguish fires, calm hatred, still winds, banish spirits, bind witches, protect friends in battle, make the dead speak, and influence love. One spell is so secret that he refused to reveal it to anyone except perhaps a beloved sister or a wife held in his arms.

These weren't simple superstitions. The Norse believed that speaking the right words in the right way while carving the right runes could actually change reality. A warrior might carve Tiwaz runes on his sword while chanting galdr to ensure victory. A woman might carve protection runes on her child's clothing. A ship owner might have runes carved on the prow to ensure safe voyages.

Runestones found throughout Scandinavia show this practice in action. Some were memorials to the dead, but they also served magical purposes. The runes themselves had power, and carving them invoked that power. A runestone might protect a bridge, mark a boundary, commemorate a hero, and invoke divine protection all at once.

The Lingsberg Runestone in Sweden.[11]

Using runes incorrectly could be dangerous. The sagas warn of people who carved runes without proper knowledge and suffered for it. In *Egil's Saga*, the hero Egil finds a young woman wasting away from illness. He discovers that a local boy carved runes for her as a love spell but made mistakes. The wrongly carved runes were making her sick instead of winning her love. Egil destroys the flawed runes, carves correct ones, and the woman recovers.

Spá was the art of prophecy and divination. A *völva* (seeress) could see the future, though what she saw was shaped by *wyrd*, the complex web of cause and effect that governed fate. Prophecy in Norse belief wasn't simple fortune-telling. It was seeing patterns, understanding how actions created consequences, and reading the threads the Norns were weaving.

Völvas were respected and feared. They traveled from community to community, performing divination rituals for those who could pay them. A household might invite a völva to learn whether crops would grow, whether children would be born healthy, or whether a planned voyage would succeed.

However, the gift of prophecy had limits. Seeing the future didn't mean you could change it. Frigg knew Baldr would die, but she couldn't prevent it. Odin knew Ragnarök was coming, but he could only prepare for it, not stop it. The Norns wove fate, and even the gods who could see their work couldn't escape it.

Útiseta ("sitting out") was a practice where someone would sit alone in isolated places, often burial mounds or in the wilderness, to commune with spirits, receive visions, or learn hidden knowledge. This was dangerous because the spirits might not be friendly, and the knowledge a person gained might drive them mad. But those willing to risk it could learn things impossible to discover otherwise. Archaeological and saga evidence suggests útiseta was practiced by both men and women.

Odin almost certainly practiced útiseta. His wandering, his time spent at boundaries and liminal spaces, and his conversations with the dead all fit the pattern. He sat on burial mounds at night, calling up spirits to question them, and traveled to the edges of the world where strange knowledge could be found.

The Norns: Weavers of Fate

At the base of Yggdrasil, beside the well of Urðr, sat three women who shaped the fate of every being in all the Nine Worlds. Their names were Urðr (Past), Verðandi (Present), and Skuld (Future). They were the Norns, and even the gods feared them.

The Norns weren't gods. They weren't exactly giants either, though some sources connect them to the jötnar. They existed outside the normal categories. They were ancient and powerful, wielding authority that even Odin couldn't challenge. What they decided happened. What they decreed couldn't be undone.

The three main Norns worked together at Yggdrasil's base. They drew water from the well of Urðr and mixed it with mud from the banks, then poured this mixture over the tree's roots to preserve it. This daily maintenance kept Yggdrasil healthy despite the constant damage from Níðhöggr's gnawing and the stags' feeding. Without the Norns' care, the World Tree would have died, and the cosmos would have collapsed.

But their primary work was weaving fate. The sources use different metaphors to describe this work. Sometimes they carve runes onto wood, sometimes they spin thread, sometimes they weave at a loom, and sometimes they simply decree what will happen. These overlapping and sometimes contradictory images all point to the same essential task: determining how long each being would live, what challenges they would face, what relationships they would form, and how they would die. Past, present, and future all existed in their work.

The word *wyrd* (Old English) or *urðr* (Old Norse) comes from a root meaning "to become" or "to turn." It wasn't a predetermined script written in advance. It was more like a web being continually woven, in which each thread connected to others and past actions created present circumstances that shaped future possibilities.

Your *ørlög* (primal law or primal layers) was the accumulated weight of your past actions, the debts you owed, the oaths you'd sworn, and the consequences of everything you'd done. Actions had consequences. What you did mattered. You couldn't escape the results of your choices.

The Norns wove these consequences into the fabric of existence. They didn't make you do things, but they determined what would result from what you did. If you swore an oath, the Norns ensured that breaking it would have consequences. If you created a debt, they saw to it that the debt would be paid.

This created a kind of limited free will. You could choose your actions, but you couldn't choose to avoid the consequences. You could decide whether to fight or flee, but once you chose, the Norns would ensure that choice played out according to the laws of cause and effect.

Every being's fate was shaped by the Norns. But that wasn't all. Norse belief also held that personal norns attended every birth, determining the fate of that specific child. These lesser norns were distinct from the three great ones at Yggdrasil, but they performed similar functions on an individual scale. When a child was born, their personal norns would come and carve or spin that child's fate.

The *Darraðarljóð*, a poem about the Battle of Clontarf, a real battle that took place in Ireland, describes Norns and Valkyries weaving fate with brutal imagery. The warp and weft of their loom are wet with blood. Spears serve as loom weights, lances as beams. Warriors split the webbing with swords while the weavers work and people die. This grim poetry captures how the Norse understood fate—not as gentle or kind, but as inevitable and often violent.

The sources describe both good and bad norns. Some granted fortunate fates, such as long life, prosperity, and honor. Others weren't so kind. The Norns could not be bargained with, bribed, or threatened. They decided what they decided, and you lived with the consequences.

The Old Norse poem "Helgakviða Hundingsbana I" describes a birth in which the Norns arrive to determine a royal child's fate. They came at night to shape his days, declaring the prince would be famous and the best of fighters. They twisted threads of fate with great power while castles crashed in Bralund. They arranged the golden strings and fastened them under the hall of the moon.

This poetic description of the Norns twisting the threads of fate and fastening them "under the hall of the moon," possibly meaning in the sky, making the child's fate part of the cosmic order, shows how seriously the Norse took this moment. Your fate was set at birth. It was woven into existence by powers beyond mortal understanding.

However, this didn't mean passivity or resignation. The Norns determined what would happen, but how you faced it was your choice. You couldn't change that you would die, but you could die with courage or cowardice, with honor or shame. That choice mattered. Your reputation, your glory, and the stories people told about you after death depended on your actions. This was the only kind of immortality humans could achieve, and they were worth more than life itself.

Archaeological evidence suggests the Norse took the Norns seriously. Grave goods often included items associated with weaving or spinning, possibly indicating the deceased's connection to fate. Some runestones invoke the Norns or use language associated with *wyrd*. The concept of fate shaped how Vikings understood both life and death.

The Norns would continue their work beyond the present age. When the gods died, when the worlds burned, when everything else was destroyed, what would happen to the Norns? The sources are silent on this point. Whether they would remain beside whatever was left of Yggdrasil, continuing to weave fate for the new world that would emerge, or whether they, too, would pass away, is left unaddressed in the surviving texts.

Chapter 4: Monsters, Giants, and Terrible Children

The Children of Loki

Loki's relationship with the giantess Angrboða produced three children who would become central to Norse mythology's apocalyptic endgame. Her name meant something like "Anguish-Bringer" or "Grief-Bringer," which should have been a warning about what their union would lead to. The offspring of Loki and Angrboða were Fenrir the wolf, Jörmungandr the serpent, and Hel, who would become queen of the dead.

The sources don't tell us much about Angrboða herself beyond her name and her role as a mother to these three beings. She lived in Járnviðr (Ironwood), a forest in Jötunheim where giantesses dwelt. The *Völuspá* mentions that "an old woman sat in Ironwood and there bred Fenrir's kin," which has led some scholars to identify this old woman as Angrboða, though the text doesn't name her explicitly. These offspring of "Fenrir's kin" included the wolves Sköll and Hati, who chase the sun and moon, though whether these were Angrboða's children or more distant descendants remains unclear.

When the gods learned about these children, they consulted prophecies. The völva's visions were clear: these three would play crucial roles in Ragnarök. The wolf would devour Odin, ending the All-Father's life. The serpent would kill Thor, poisoning the god who had protected Midgard for ages. The daughter would open her realm to armies of the dead, providing forces for the final battle.

Odin decided to deal with the problem. He sent gods to Járnviðr to bring Loki's children to Asgard.

Jörmungandr the World Serpent

The serpent was still young when the gods seized him, but he was already massive and still growing rapidly. Odin threw Jörmungandr into the ocean surrounding Midgard.

The serpent landed in the deep sea, where he continued growing. He grew until he became so enormous that he encircled the entire world. His body formed a living boundary around Midgard, and eventually, he grew large enough to bite his own tail, creating an unbroken ring around the realm of humans. This made Jörmungandr into the Miðgarðsormr, the Midgard Serpent.

Thor and Jörmungandr were destined enemies. They would meet several times before Ragnarök, and each encounter nearly ended in disaster. The most famous involved Thor going fishing with the giant Hymir, which we will discuss in detail in Chapter 5. What matters for now is that Odin's decision to throw the serpent into the ocean didn't eliminate the threat; it just moved Jörmungandr to a place where he could grow undisturbed until the final battle.

At Ragnarök, Jörmungandr would emerge from the ocean and come ashore, venom dripping from his fangs, poisoning the sky and earth. He would fight Thor in their final confrontation. Thor would kill the serpent with Mjölnir but then stagger back nine paces and fall dead himself, poisoned by Jörmungandr's venom. They would destroy each other, fulfilling the prophecy that bound them together.

Hel, Queen of the Dead

The daughter of Loki and Angrboða was described as half-alive and half-dead or half flesh-colored and half blue-black. Her appearance was unsettling, as it was a visible manifestation of her connection to death. She was neither fully alive nor completely dead.

Odin sent Hel to Niflheim and gave her authority there. Snorri's description mentions nine realms in connection with her rule, though scholars debate whether this means nine distinct sections of the underworld or simply emphasizes the extent of her domain. She became the queen of those who died of sickness, old age, and accidents. Her realm, Helheim, was cold and misty, located in or near Niflheim, where the primordial ice still lingered.

Helheim wasn't a place of punishment in the Christian sense of eternal torment for sins. It wasn't quite hell, though later Christian scribes couldn't resist making connections and may have shaped some descriptions to emphasize similarities. Helheim was simply where most people went when they died. If you didn't die gloriously in battle and weren't chosen by the Valkyries for Valhalla or by Freyja for Fólkvangr, you went to Hel's realm. This made Hel's domain far more populous than Valhalla. Most deaths weren't heroic. Most people died in their beds or from illness rather than in combat.

The dead in Helheim are described in the sources as pale shadows, drained of color. They dwelt in a realm of fog and cold. The sources provide limited detail about their existence there, focusing more on the physical description of the realm itself than on the experience of its inhabitants.

Hel's hall was called Éljúðnir (Misery). The sources describe it as having high walls and enormous gates, with a threshold called Fallandaforad (Falling-Peril or Stumbling-Block) that made entry difficult. Inside, Hel had a bed called Kör (Sickbed), a table called Hungr (Hunger), and a knife called Sultr (Starvation). Even her servants had ominous names: Ganglati (Lazy Walker) and Ganglöt (Lazy), suggesting slow, reluctant service. Everything about her realm emphasized its connection to decline, decay, and the negative aspects of existence.

Yet Helheim had its own order and rules. Hel herself wasn't depicted as cruel or actively malevolent. She ruled her realm, hosted the dead, and maintained the boundary between life and death. She represented death's inevitability and finality, but she didn't torture the dead or seek to expand her domain through violence.

The path to Helheim was dangerous and difficult. Those who journeyed there while still alive had to cross the river Gjöll on a bridge called Gjallarbrú, guarded by a giantess named Móðguðr. Then they had to pass through gates guarded by the massive hound Garmr, who would attack anyone trying to leave Helheim without permission. The journey was meant to be one-way. You could go to Hel's realm, but you couldn't easily return.

Hel rarely appears in the myths beyond her role as keeper of the dead. When Baldr died, the gods sent a messenger named Hermóðr to Helheim to try to bring him back. Hel set a condition for his release: if everything in the Nine Worlds wept for Baldr, she would release him. If even one thing refused to weep, he would remain in her realm. This condition seemed simple, but it proved impossible to fulfill. One giantess, probably Loki in disguise, refused to weep, and Baldr stayed dead.

At Ragnarök, Hel would provide forces for the battle against the gods. The dead would rise from her realm and join Loki's army. A ship called Naglfar, built from the fingernails and toenails of the dead—which is why proper funeral preparations included trimming the nails of corpses since every untrimmed nail contributed to Naglfar's construction—would carry armies of the dead to the battlefield. Hel's realm would open, and the dead would march out, swelling the ranks of those fighting against the gods.

Fenrir the Wolf

Fenrir was different from his siblings. Where Jörmungandr was thrown into the ocean and Hel was sent to rule the dead, Fenrir was kept in Asgard. The gods thought they could raise him, making him easier to control when he got older. They kept him contained while he was still young. This decision would prove to be one of their greatest mistakes.

Only Týr, the god of war and justice, was brave enough to feed Fenrir. Every day, Týr would bring food to the wolf, getting close enough to this growing predator to place meat within reach of his jaws. The other gods watched Fenrir grow larger and stronger every day, and they became increasingly nervous.

Fenrir grew at an alarming rate. What had been a manageable wolf cub became a massive beast whose jaws could snap trees and whose strength exceeded even Thor's. The prophecies were clear about Fenrir's ultimate fate. He would break free from whatever bound him, devour Odin at Ragnarök, and be one of the primary forces destroying the cosmic order.

The gods decided they needed to bind Fenrir before he became too powerful to restrain. They couldn't kill him since that would violate the laws of hospitality. They had brought him into Asgard themselves, and they would be breaking the oaths they had made by taking him in. The sources also tell us the gods did not want to stain their holy places with his blood. They needed another solution.

They approached Fenrir with what they framed as a test of strength. They had forged a chain called Læðingr and challenged Fenrir to try breaking it. If he could break free, it would prove his great strength. Fenrir agreed. He was young and confident, and he saw no reason to refuse a challenge that would demonstrate his power.

The gods bound him with Læðingr. Fenrir flexed and strained, and the chain snapped apart like thread. The gods pretended to be impressed while privately panicking. They needed a stronger chain.

They forged Drómi, a chain twice as strong as Læðingr. Again, they challenged Fenrir to a test of strength. And again, he agreed. They bound him with Drómi. This time, Fenrir had to work harder to break free. He strained and struggled, his muscles bulging, his legs driving against the ground. Then Drómi shattered, links flying in all directions.

Fenrir was pleased with himself. He had proven his strength twice, demonstrating that no chain the gods could forge would hold him. The gods congratulated him while frantically trying to figure out their next move.

They turned to the dwarves, the master craftsmen who could forge items the gods themselves couldn't create. They commissioned an unbreakable binding, and the dwarves delivered Gleipnir.

Gleipnir didn't look impressive. It appeared to be a simple ribbon, smooth and soft, almost silken in texture. But it was made from six seemingly impossible things: the sound of a cat's footfall, the beard of a woman, the roots of a mountain, the sinews of a bear, the breath of a fish, and the spittle of a bird. Because these things don't exist, the ribbon created from them couldn't be broken by physical force. It existed outside the normal rules of strength and resistance.

The gods brought Gleipnir to Fenrir and challenged him to test his strength against this ribbon. Fenrir looked at it and immediately became suspicious. Why would the gods want him to struggle against something so weak-looking? Why would they travel to the dwarves for a simple ribbon? This had to be a trick.

Fenrir said he would let them bind him with Gleipnir, but only if one of the gods would place their hand in his mouth as a pledge of good faith. If this were a genuine test and he could break free, fine. But if this were an attempt to bind him permanently, he would take someone's hand as compensation for their betrayal.

The gods looked at each other. None of them wanted to volunteer their hand to a wolf whose jaws could crush stone. They all knew what would happen if Gleipnir worked as intended. Fenrir wouldn't be able to break free, and whoever put their hand in his mouth would lose it.

Only Týr stepped forward. He was the god of law and oaths, the one who embodied justice and keeping one's word. He had been feeding

Fenrir all this time, developing a relationship with the wolf. And he understood that someone had to make this sacrifice if they were going to bind the greatest threat to Asgard's survival.

Týr placed his right hand between Fenrir's jaws.

The gods bound Fenrir with Gleipnir, wrapping the ribbon around the wolf's body multiple times. Fenrir tried to break free. He strained and struggled, using all his enormous strength, the same strength that had snapped Læðingr and Drómi like thread. His muscles bulged. His legs pushed against the ground with enough force to crack stone. He threw his whole body against the binding, trying to tear it apart through sheer power.

The ribbon didn't break. It didn't even stretch. The more Fenrir struggled, the tighter Gleipnir became, binding him more securely with each movement.

Fenrir bit down with all his strength, his massive jaws closing on Týr's wrist. The god's hand was severed cleanly, blood spurting as Týr stumbled back, clutching the stump. Týr screamed in pain, but he didn't try to retrieve his hand. The other gods considered this an acceptable price. They had bound the wolf, preventing the immediate threat to Asgard. One god's hand seemed a fair trade for their collective safety.

The gods took the bound wolf to an island called Lyngvi in the lake Ámsvartnir. This wasn't a random location. Lyngvi was isolated, surrounded by deep water that would prevent anyone from easily reaching the wolf. The lake's name, Ámsvartnir, meant something like "Ember Black" or "Coal Black," suggesting dark, deep waters that would deter rescue attempts.

On the island, the gods performed the final binding. They passed a cord called Gelgja through a massive stone slab called Gjöll. This wasn't just rope. Gelgja was magical, as it was strong enough to hold the ribbon that held Fenrir. They drove Gjöll deep into the earth with another stone called Þviti, which they hammered down like a stake, anchoring the whole thing together so securely that no amount of struggling could dislodge it.

Then came the final cruelty. They took a sword—the sources don't say whose sword it was—and propped it vertically between Fenrir's jaws. The hilt was braced against his lower jaw, the point against his upper jaw, keeping his mouth forced open at an angle that prevented him from closing it.

Fenrir couldn't close his mouth. He couldn't bite. He couldn't speak, only howl and snarl around the blade. Saliva poured from his open jaws in a constant stream, so much that it formed a river flowing from his mouth. The sources name this river Ván. Fenrir would remain there, bound to the stone, mouth propped open by a sword, drooling a river, unable to move or speak or do anything but wait until Ragnarök. The gods left him there and returned to Asgard, satisfied that they had solved the problem of Loki's dangerous son.

When Ragnarök came, Fenrir would break free from Gleipnir. The sources describe the earth shaking, trees being uprooted, and mountains falling as the wolf struggled against his bonds. Finally, the ribbon would snap. Fenrir would shake himself free and run across the battlefield with his jaws open from earth to sky.

He would find Odin and devour the All-Father. Odin, who had orchestrated Fenrir's binding, who had known this fate was coming, would be swallowed by the wolf he had imprisoned. But Fenrir's victory would be brief. Odin's son Víðarr would approach the wolf and place one foot on his lower jaw, wearing a special shoe made from all the leather scraps ever discarded by shoemakers collected over all of time. He would grab the upper jaw and tear Fenrir apart, avenging his father.

All three of Loki's children would die at Ragnarök after helping to destroy the gods. The prophecies would be fulfilled. The cosmic order would fall. And then, perhaps, something new would begin.

Jötunheim: Life Among the Giants

The English word "giant" creates misleading expectations. When we hear "giant," we think of enormous beings, massive creatures towering over normal humans. Some jötnar fit this description. There were jötnar who were physically huge, mountain-sized beings who shook the earth when they walked. Þjazi could transform into an eagle large enough to carry off a goddess. Hrungnir was described as the strongest of all giants, with a head and heart made of stone. Hymir was so large that when Thor caught Jörmungandr while fishing, the giant's boat seemed tiny in comparison to the serpent.

But many jötnar appeared as normal-sized beings, no larger than gods or humans, and some were even described as beautiful. Gerðr shone with light when she moved. Skaði was formidable and attractive enough that the gods competed to marry her, or at least didn't object when she demanded to choose a husband. The giantess Gunnlöð, who guarded the Mead of Poetry, was beautiful enough that Odin seduced her to gain access to the mead.

What made someone a jötunn wasn't size. Scholars have suggested that jötnar represented the wilderness and the untamed aspects of nature, powers that existed before the gods created order in the cosmos. This would explain why gods and giants had such complicated relationships. The jötnar weren't simply enemies. They were forces that couldn't be eliminated without eliminating nature itself.

The word jötunn is often interpreted as meaning "devourer" or "glutton," though the etymology is debated. What's clearer is their role in the cosmic structure. They lived in Jötunheim, a realm of harsh, wild terrain. But they weren't mindless monsters. They had their own society, their own kings and hierarchies, and their own halls and treasures.

Jötunheim's geography varied widely. Some parts were frozen wastelands of ice and snow, harsh enough that even giants found them challenging. Other areas were rocky mountains with peaks that scraped the sky. They were dangerous to climb and impossible to farm. Dense forests covered other regions, dark woods where paths didn't exist, and travelers could wander lost for years. Rivers ran through Jötunheim, but they were dangerous. Some carried poison, and others flowed with such force that crossing them meant risking death.

Despite the harsh environment, giants built halls and settlements that showed significant architectural and cultural sophistication. These weren't crude caves or primitive encampments. Giants constructed halls that rivaled or exceeded those in Asgard in size and grandeur.

Útgarða-Loki ruled over a hall so large that Thor and his companions couldn't see the back wall when they entered. The hall contained multiple chambers, countless servants, and enough space to host tests of strength.

Þrymr the giant had a hall grand enough to host what he believed would be a wedding feast for all the important beings in Jötunheim. He sat on his high seat and commanded servants to prepare for Freyja's arrival. When Thor arrived disguised as the bride, the feast included massive amounts of food and mead, demonstrating both wealth and hospitality on a scale that matched Asgard's own celebrations.

Geirröðr lived in a hall with high seats, multiple chambers, and various magical implements. He had daughters who practiced magic and servants who obeyed his commands. His hall included spaces for hosting guests, even if he intended to kill them, demonstrating that giants understood and followed codes of hospitality even when they planned treachery.

The sources mention giant kings who ruled over territories and giants gathering for feasts and events. The extent of formal political structures is largely inferred by scholars based on these scattered references rather than explicitly described in the myths themselves.

Giants practiced magic. Many giantesses were skilled in seiðr and prophecy. The völva who speaks in the *Völuspá*, revealing the cosmos's secrets from creation through Ragnarök, appears to be a giantess. Giants knew runes and galdr. They could shapeshift, brew magical concoctions, and cast curses that even gods feared. Their magical knowledge sometimes exceeded the gods' own, which is why figures like Odin traveled to Jötunheim seeking wisdom.

Of course, the gods and jötnar were enemies. Thor spent much of his time killing giants who threatened Asgard or Midgard, and many myths involve gods tricking, robbing, or defeating giants through strength or cunning. The constant threat of giants attacking Asgard motivated many divine decisions, from building protective walls to gathering armies for Ragnarök. Giants were often portrayed as opponents to be overcome and threats to be defeated.

But they were also family in the most literal sense. Odin's mother was the giantess Bestla, daughter of the giant Bölþorn. This made Odin himself part giant. Thor's mother was Jörð (Earth), often identified as a giantess, making Thor descended from the jötnar he spent his time fighting. The gods' family trees were intertwined with giant lineages in ways that complicated any simple us-versus-them narrative.

Marriage alliances between gods and giants were common. Freyr married Gerðr after his servant threatened her with terrible curses. Njörðr married Skaði as compensation for the gods killing her father. Odin had relationships with various giantesses beyond his marriage to Frigg. These weren't all political marriages or forced arrangements. Some seem to have involved genuine attraction or love, while others were clearly transactional.

The children of these unions were fully accepted as gods despite their mixed heritage. Nobody questioned Odin's legitimacy because his mother was a giant. Thor was the most popular god among the Vikings despite being half-giant himself. The boundary between divine and giant wasn't determined by parentage but by allegiance and nature, which side you fought for, which realm you called home, and which values you embodied.

Giants and gods traded with each other, made treaties, and sometimes cooperated when mutual interests aligned. When the gods needed certain kinds of knowledge, they went to the giants who possessed it. When they needed specific magical items that even dwarves couldn't create, they sometimes turned to giant craftsmen or sorcerers. When they wanted to learn certain forms of magic, they found giant teachers.

They attended each other's feasts, though usually with suspicion and often with hidden motives. The god Ægir, who might have been a giant or a being between categories, hosted feasts for both gods and giants. These gatherings sometimes turned violent, but they happened regularly enough to constitute normal diplomatic interaction.

Some giants were wise counselors whom even Odin respected. Vafþrúðnir challenged Odin to a contest of wisdom where they would trade questions and answers about the cosmos's deepest secrets. The questions covered creation, the nature of the worlds, the fates of gods and giants, and obscure knowledge about beings and places. Vafþrúðnir lost only when Odin asked a question that only the All-Father could answer. "What did Odin whisper in Baldr's ear before Baldr was placed on the funeral pyre?" Since only Odin knew this, Vafþrúðnir couldn't answer and lost the contest. But until that final question, the giant had matched Odin's knowledge point for point, demonstrating wisdom that rivaled even the wisest of gods.

Mímir, whose head Odin preserved after the Æsir-Vanir War, was a giant whose wisdom exceeded even Vafþrúðnir's. Odin consulted Mímir's severed head when he needed counsel on matters too complex or important for other advisors. The fact that Odin's most trusted advisor was a giant's head says something about where true wisdom could be found.

Other giants were craftsmen whose skills benefited the gods. The giant who built Asgard's wall was hired for his exceptional ability. He could work stone and construct fortifications better than anyone the gods knew. His work was so good that the gods panicked when they realized he might actually complete the impossible task on time and claim his payment. They had to resort to trickery to prevent him from finishing, but they kept his work, acknowledging its quality even as they cheated him of payment.

Giants could be generous hosts. Some offered hospitality to traveling gods, providing food and shelter in accordance with the laws of hospitality. When the gods violated these laws by stealing, killing hosts, or breaking oaths, they acted dishonorably.

But giants could also be genuinely dangerous. Þjazi kidnapped Iðunn, threatening all the gods with rapid aging. Þrymr stole Thor's hammer and tried to blackmail the gods into giving him Freyja. Some giants even wanted to destroy the cosmic order entirely.

This created a cosmos where boundaries remained permeable. A giant could ally with the gods. A god could have giant parents or marry into giant families. The conflict wasn't between good and evil but between order and the forces outside that order. Some giants were enemies who had to be fought. Others were allies, family members, teachers, or simply beings living their own lives in their own realm.

The gods understood this complexity even as they fought giants. Thor killed countless jötnar, but he also drank with them and accepted their hospitality. Odin wandered through Jötunheim seeking their wisdom. Freyr loved a giant woman enough to give up his sword for her.

At Ragnarök, this complex relationship would fail entirely.

The Dwarves: The Cosmic Engineers

The dwarves' origin story is deeply weird and somewhat disturbing. According to the traditional sources, they were created from maggots, specifically the maggots that formed in Ymir's flesh after Odin and his brothers killed the primordial giant and used his body to build the cosmos.

These maggots had been feeding on Ymir's decomposing corpse when the gods noticed them. Rather than destroying them, the gods transformed them into dwarves and endowed them with human-like intelligence and understanding.

Dwarves lived beneath mountains and inside the earth itself in vast halls carved from stone. Some traditions place their homeland in Svartálfheim, the realm of the dark elves, with sources often treating dark elves and dwarves as the same beings or closely related. They rarely came to the surface, and when they did, they had to be careful.

According to some traditions, dwarves turned to stone if caught by sunlight. The *Alvíssmál*, from the *Poetic Edda*, tells of a dwarf named Alvíss, meaning "All-Wise," who came to claim Thor's daughter as his bride. Thor delayed him by asking question after question about the kennings, the poetic names for things, forcing Alvíss to demonstrate his vast knowledge. The dwarf answered every question correctly, but Thor kept him talking until dawn. When the first rays of sunlight struck him, Alvíss turned to stone, frozen forever.

This vulnerability made the dwarves creatures of darkness and the underground. Their halls were lit by forge fires and glowing crystals rather than by the sun or the moon. They worked in the deep places where stone and metal could be found, crafting without fear of dawn.

And craft they did. Dwarves were the greatest craftsmen in all the Nine Worlds, surpassing even the gods in their ability to forge magical objects. Their skill with metal, stone, and enchantment made them essential to the cosmic order despite their origin from maggots.

The sources preserve the names of several groups of dwarf craftsmen. The sons of Ívaldi created some of the gods' most important treasures. Brokkr and Eitri (also called Sindri in some sources) forged treasures in a famous competition. These were master artisans capable of creating objects that defied the natural law.

One night, Loki broke into Thor and Sif's bedroom while they slept. He crept to Sif's bedside with shears and cut off all her beautiful golden hair, leaving her nearly bald.

Why? The sources do not say. Maybe he thought it would be funny. Maybe he was bored. Maybe he was drunk. Loki did not always need good reasons to do what he did.

When Sif woke and saw what had been done, her screams woke Thor. And when Thor realized what Loki had done to his wife, his rage was volcanic. He found Loki and grabbed him by the throat, fully intending to break every bone in the trickster's body.

Loki, choking and terrified, managed to gasp out a promise. He would get the dwarves to make new hair for Sif, hair of real gold that would grow like natural hair. The best craftsmen in all the Nine Worlds would forge it. Thor, still furious but willing to see whether Loki could actually fix what he had done, released him. But the threat was clear. If Loki failed, Thor would kill him.

Loki traveled to Svartálfheim and found the sons of Ívaldi, the most skilled dwarf craftsmen he knew. He explained what he needed. They could do it, they said, but the work would be difficult and expensive. Loki, desperate to save his own life, promised them fame and recognition. And while they were at it, he suggested, why not make a few other treasures? Gifts for the other gods would help smooth things over. Perhaps a spear for Odin? A ship for Freyr?

The sons of Ívaldi agreed. They forged three masterworks: golden hair that would grow naturally once attached to Sif's head, Gungnir, the spear that never missed, and Skíðblaðnir, the ship that could hold all the gods yet fold small enough to fit in a pocket.

Loki returned to Asgard with these treasures. Sif got her new hair. Odin received Gungnir. Runes carved into its point ensured not just a hit but a killing blow. Odin could cast Gungnir over an army to claim their deaths for himself, marking them for Valhalla or sealing their doom. The spear symbolized his authority as both a war god and a king. Freyr received Skíðblaðnir. Whenever its sail was raised, it caught favorable wind regardless of direction. Its size shifting and weather mastery made it invaluable.

The crisis was resolved. Loki had fixed his mistake. But Loki could not leave it alone.

On his way back from Svartálfheim, he encountered another pair of dwarf smiths, Brokkr and his brother Eitri. Loki, feeling pleased with himself and unable to resist stirring up trouble, made them an offer. He bet his own head that these two smiths could not create three treasures as fine as the ones the sons of Ívaldi had just made.

Brokkr and Eitri looked at each other. Then they looked at Loki. This arrogant god was wagering his head that they, master craftsmen, could not match another workshop's output?

They accepted. Brokkr and Eitri returned to their forge. Eitri explained that he would shape the items, but Brokkr had to work the bellows without stopping, not even for a moment. The slightest interruption would ruin everything.

First, they forged Gullinbursti. Eitri placed the pigskin in the forge and began working it with hammer and magic. Brokkr worked the bellows, pumping steadily to keep the fire at exactly the right temperature.

Loki, watching from the shadows, realized he was about to lose his head unless he did something. He transformed into a fly and landed on Brokkr's hand. Then he bit down, hard enough to draw blood.

The pain was intense. Blood welled up where the fly had bitten. But Brokkr had given his word. He kept pumping, and the rhythm never faltered.

When Eitri finally called him to stop, they pulled from the forge a living boar made of gold, its bristles glowing with their own light. This was Gullinbursti. It could run through air and water faster than any horse, and its golden bristles shone brightly enough to pierce darkness and fog. Freyr could ride it anywhere, across any terrain.

Next came Draupnir. Eitri placed gold in the forge and began the shaping. Brokkr returned to the bellows.

Loki, as a fly, bit Brokkr's neck this time, biting harder and drawing more blood. The pain was worse. Blood ran down Brokkr's neck and stained his shirt. But Brokkr did not stop. His hands kept moving. The bellows kept pumping.

When Eitri removed the ring from the forge, it was perfect. Every ninth night, it would produce eight new gold rings of equal weight, ensuring perpetual wealth.

Now Loki was desperate. They had already created two perfect treasures. One more and he would lose his head, literally.

For the final item, Eitri placed iron in the forge. This would be the greatest work: Mjölnir, a weapon unlike any other. The shaping required absolute precision. The bellows had to maintain a perfect temperature. Any interruption at all would be disastrous.

Brokkr began pumping. Loki transformed into a fly again, knowing this was his last chance. He landed on Brokkr's eyelid and bit as hard as he could, biting deep and tearing the flesh.

Blood poured into Brokkr's eye. He could not see, and the pain was excruciating. For just one moment, one single instant, Brokkr stopped pumping to wipe the blood away.

That moment was enough.

When Eitri removed Mjölnir from the forge, the hammer was magnificent, perfect in every way but one: the handle was too short. That single moment of interrupted bellows work had prevented the handle from reaching its proper length.

The treasures were brought before the gods for judgment. There were six items: three from the sons of Ívaldi, three from Brokkr and Eitri. The gods examined them all. They tested them. And then they debated.

Eventually, they rendered their verdict. Mjölnir was the greatest treasure ever made. Despite its shortened handle, the hammer could defend Asgard against any threat. It always struck its target and always returned to Thor's hand after being thrown. It shattered giants' skulls and crushed mountains, and its impact echoed across the worlds. It could also consecrate marriages, births, and funerals, making it sacred as well as deadly. Its abilities outweighed everything else. Brokkr and Eitri had won.

Brokkr turned to Loki and demanded his head.

Loki smiled. "The wager," he said carefully, "was for my head. You can have my head. But the wager said nothing about my neck. You are welcome to take my head, but you cannot cut through my neck to remove it."

Brokkr, furious at being cheated by trickster logic, decided on a different punishment. If he could not cut off Loki's head, he would at least shut his lying mouth. He took an awl and pierced Loki's lips, then threaded them together with a leather cord, sewing Loki's mouth shut.

For a while, Loki could not speak. Eventually, he tore the stitching out, ripping his own lips open to free his mouth. But he had learned something. Even clever words and careful loopholes had limits. And dwarves remembered being cheated.

This story reveals several important things about dwarves. They were proud of their craft and willing to compete to prove their skill. They took oaths seriously. They had leverage since the gods needed their creations. And they could be vindictive when cheated.

Dwarves understood runes and could carve them to activate their creations. They knew magical formulas that transformed objects into weapons that never missed or ships that defied natural laws. By the time the major treasures were forged, dwarves could combine metalwork with runic magic to create items that operated according to their own laws.

They also knew the value of their work and did not give it away cheaply. When gods came to commission items, dwarves demanded real payment, magical objects in trade, rare materials, or significant favors.

The relationship between gods and dwarves was transactional but respectful. Gods did not command dwarves. They negotiated as equals, recognizing that dwarves possessed skills the gods needed and could not replicate. The gods' power depended on dwarven-forged items, which gave dwarves significant leverage.

At Ragnarök, what happened to the dwarves remains unknown. Perhaps they continued living in the deep places where gods and giants could not reach them.

Chapter 5: Adventures and Misadventures

Thor's Fishing Trip

One day, Thor traveled to Jötunheim. *Hymiskviða*, the poem that tells this story, does not explain Thor's reasons for being in the giants' territory or how he ended up at Hymir's hall. Thor arrived at the giant's home and stayed the night. Hymir was described as one of the strongest and most impressive giants. He was known for owning enormous cattle and for his skill at fishing in the deep ocean, where the largest creatures dwelled.

The next morning, Hymir prepared to go fishing. Thor announced he would come along. Hymir looked at Thor and expressed doubt about whether this visitor would be any use on a fishing expedition to the deep ocean. The journey would be long, the waters dangerous, and the work hard. Could Thor handle it?

Thor's response was to assert that he could row farther out to sea and stay out longer than Hymir could manage. This was Thor's pride speaking, his unwillingness to be seen as weak or incapable. Hymir accepted the boast without arguing. If Thor wanted to come, he could come. But he would need bait.

Hymir told Thor to get his own bait from the giant's herd. Thor went to Hymir's cattle and selected the largest, finest ox in the entire herd, a beast called Himinhrjótr ("Heaven-Bellower" or "Sky-Bellower"), named for its tremendous size and the volume of its bellowing. Thor walked up to this massive animal, grabbed its head with his bare hands, and twisted.

The ox's head ripped off in Thor's grip. He brought it back to the boat, casually carrying the head of Hymir's finest ox as bait.

Hymir was disturbed by this casual destruction of such a valuable animal, but they got in the boat and began rowing out to sea.

Hymir rowed them to the fishing grounds where he usually caught whales. He prepared to stop there and start fishing, but Thor kept rowing. Hymir warned him that going farther out was dangerous and that they would disturb Jörmungandr, the World Serpent, who lay coiled at the bottom of the ocean. Thor ignored the warning and kept rowing anyway.

When they were far out over the deepest part of the ocean, Thor finally stopped. He baited his hook with the ox's head, using the entire massive skull as bait. Then he cast his line into the depths.

Jörmungandr took the bait.

The World Serpent bit down on the ox's head, and Thor's hook caught in the serpent's jaw. Thor began hauling on the line. The serpent, realizing it was caught, tried to dive deeper, pulling against the line with all its massive strength. Thor just pulled harder.

This was a contest between the god's strength and the serpent's size. Thor's feet pressed down against the bottom of the boat with such force that they went straight through the wood. He was standing on the ocean floor while still in the boat, using the sea bottom for leverage as he hauled on the line.

The serpent rose from the depths. Its head broke the surface, venom dripping from its fangs, its eyes full of hatred for the god who'd hooked it. Thor and Jörmungandr faced each other across the water, enemies who would one day kill each other at Ragnarök.

Thor grabbed Mjölnir, ready to smash the serpent's skull and kill it. If he succeeded, one of the three greatest threats to Asgard would be eliminated.

But Hymir panicked. He saw the serpent rising, saw Thor about to strike it, and, in his fear, he cut the fishing line with his knife.

Jörmungandr sank back into the ocean depths, the hook still in its jaw. Some versions say Thor struck Hymir or knocked him overboard in anger at the interference.

However, the fishing trip was not the end of Thor's visit to Hymir's hall. What happened next showed Thor's strength in a different way.

The giants at Hymir's hall held a feast, and Thor drank heavily from their cups. One of the giants, perhaps Hymir's wife or another relative, grew tired of Thor's presence and wanted him gone. She suggested a test. Thor should try to break Hymir's goblet.

This seemed simple enough. Thor took the goblet—a massive drinking vessel made of enchanted glass or crystal—and hurled it against a stone pillar. The pillar shattered, but the goblet remained intact.

He threw it against the stone floor. The floor cracked. The goblet did not.

He then smashed it against the walls, against the benches, against every hard surface in the hall. Nothing worked. The goblet was indestructible.

Then someone—different versions disagree on who—whispered advice to Thor. There was one thing harder than the enchanted goblet: Hymir's own skull. The giant's head was harder than stone, harder than any material in his hall. If Thor wanted to break the goblet, he would have to smash it against Hymir's head.

Thor walked up to Hymir, who was sitting, enjoying the feast. Without warning, Thor smashed the goblet against the giant's skull as hard as he could.

The goblet shattered into pieces.

Hymir's skull remained undamaged. The giant sat there, probably with a headache, while fragments of his prized goblet scattered across the floor.

Having broken the supposedly unbreakable goblet, Thor had proven his point. But he had not come to Hymir's hall just to fish and break cups. The gods had sent him there for a reason: they needed Hymir's massive brewing cauldron.

The gods wanted to hold a great feast, but they lacked a cauldron large enough to brew ale for all of them. Hymir owned such a cauldron. It was one mile deep and large enough to brew beer for all the gods at once. Thor demanded it.

Hymir, having just watched Thor knock him into the ocean, smash his prized goblet against his own skull, and generally make a nuisance of himself, was reluctant to hand over his valuable cauldron. He told Thor he could take it—if he could carry it.

Thor grabbed the cauldron by the rim and tried to lift it. It would not budge. He tried again, straining with all his divine strength. The cauldron shifted slightly but would not come off the ground.

Finally, Thor heaved with everything he had. The cauldron came up. He lifted it over his head and carried it out of the hall, his feet breaking through the floor with each step from the enormous weight.

Thor and Útgarða-Loki

Thor's journey to Útgarða-Loki's hall is one of the stranger stories in Norse mythology, featuring tricks, illusions, and Thor being repeatedly defeated by clever magic and misdirection.

Thor set out from Asgard with Loki as his companion. They traveled through Midgard, heading toward Jötunheim. On the first night, they stopped at a farm and asked for hospitality. The farmer and his wife welcomed them, as the laws of hospitality demanded, but they were poor and had little food to offer two hungry travelers.

Thor solved this problem in his characteristic, direct manner. He killed his two goats, Tanngrisnir and Tanngnjóstr, the same goats that pulled his chariot. He butchered them quickly, cooked the meat, and shared it with the farmer's family. Before they began eating, Thor told them to throw all the bones into the goatskins when they were done eating. They were not to break any of the bones or damage them in any way. All they had to do was place them carefully in the skins.

The farmer, his wife, and their two children, Þjálfi and Röskva, ate gratefully. The goat meat was delicious, and there was more food than they had seen in months. But Þjálfi, the son, was so hungry, and the marrow inside the bones looked so appealing, that he cracked open one of the leg bones with his knife and sucked out the marrow inside. He was careful to put the broken bone back in the goatskin afterward, hoping no one would notice.

When morning came, Thor took Mjölnir and blessed the goatskins, speaking words of power over them. The goats came back to life, flesh reforming around the bones, hide covering the muscle, until they stood whole and alive again. However, one of them was limping badly on the leg where Þjálfi had cracked the bone. The magical resurrection had worked, but the broken bone had not healed properly, leaving the goat permanently lame.

Thor saw this, and his eyes blazed with anger. His face turned red. His knuckles turned white as he gripped Mjölnir's handle so hard that the muscles in his forearms stood out. The farmer and his family thought they were about to die. They had violated Thor's explicit instructions, damaged his property, and now the god of thunder was about to kill them all for it.

The farmer threw himself and his family on Thor's mercy, offering everything he owned as compensation. Thor's anger cooled somewhat. The farmer had nothing of value to give, so he offered his two children instead. Thor accepted Þjálfi and his sister Röskva as his servants who would serve him as long as he required. With this debt paid, Thor left the lame goat with the farmer and continued his journey with Loki and his two new servants.

The four travelers continued toward Jötunheim. As night fell, they found themselves in a forest, where they found what seemed to be a huge hall with an enormous entrance. They went inside to sleep, finding the hall oddly shaped with a large side chamber. During the night, they felt the ground shake with earthquakes and heard tremendous roaring. They huddled in the side chamber, frightened but unable to see what was causing the disturbance.

When morning came, they went outside and found a giant asleep nearby. He was enormous, larger than any giant they had seen before. The roaring sounds had been his snoring. The earthquakes had been him shifting in his sleep. And the "hall" they had slept in was actually his glove; the side chamber had been the thumb.

The giant woke and introduced himself as Skrýmir, meaning "Big Fellow." He offered to travel with them toward Útgarðr, which was where they were heading. Skrýmir was friendly but casual about his size and strength in ways that made Thor uncomfortable. When they stopped to eat, Skrýmir tied all their provisions into his food sack and carried it.

That night, Skrýmir went to sleep under an oak tree and immediately began snoring so loudly that the ground shook. Thor, Þjálfi, and Röskva tried to sleep but could not with the noise. They tried to wake Skrýmir but failed. Thor tried to open Skrýmir's food sack to get their provisions, but the knots were tied in a way he could not undo.

Frustrated and angry, Thor took Mjölnir and struck Skrýmir on the head. The giant stirred slightly and asked if a leaf had fallen on his head. Thor was stunned. He had hit the giant with his hammer, and Skrýmir had felt it as barely a tickle.

Later in the night, Thor tried again, hitting Skrýmir even harder. The giant woke slightly and asked if an acorn had fallen on his head. Thor was amazed that his hammer strikes were having no effect.

Just before dawn, Thor hit Skrýmir a third time with all his strength, driving Mjölnir so hard into the giant's forehead that the hammer sank in to the handle. Skrýmir sat up and brushed at his forehead, commenting that a bird must have dropped some twigs on him.

Morning came, and Skrýmir told them he was heading north. Útgarðr lay to the east. He gave them directions and one warning: the people in Útgarða-Loki's hall would think they were small. They should not brag or boast about their abilities because the giants there were much greater than they were. Then Skrýmir left; the sources note that Thor was quite happy to see him go.

They reached Útgarðr and found a massive hall with enormous gates. They squeezed through the bars of the gate—it was so large that they could walk between the bars rather than needing to open it. Inside, they found giants sitting on benches. All of them were huge.

They approached the high seat where Útgarða-Loki sat. He was the king of this place, and he was clearly powerful and confident. When he noticed the newcomers, he did not look impressed. In fact, he seemed amused. He made mocking comments about Thor being smaller than expected, asking if this was really the famous Thor they had heard so much about. He wondered aloud if Thor was perhaps still just a boy, as he seemed too young to compete with real warriors.

Thor bristled at these insults. His pride would not let such mockery go unanswered. Útgarða-Loki laughed. He said if Thor and his companions could demonstrate skills greater than anyone in the hall in any contest of their choosing, they would be proven worthy and welcome. Otherwise, they should leave rather than embarrass themselves further. No one could stay in Útgarðr who could not prove they excelled at something.

Loki spoke up first, unable to contain himself after the long journey and meager rations. He claimed no one present could eat faster than he could. He was ravenously hungry, so he was confident he could out-eat anyone the giants put forward.

Útgarða-Loki accepted the challenge and called forward a giant named Logi. Servants brought out a massive wooden trough filled with meat and placed it between Loki and Logi. The rules were simple. They would start at opposite ends and eat toward the middle. Whoever consumed more would win.

They began. Loki ate with desperate speed, tearing meat from bones and swallowing as fast as he could. He ate like someone starving. He consumed huge quantities of meat at an impressive pace, thinking he was winning easily.

They met in the middle of the trough. But when they examined the results, Logi had eaten not just the meat but also the bones, gristle, and even the wooden trough itself. Logi had consumed everything in his path, leaving nothing behind. Loki had lost badly.

Þjálfi spoke up next, claiming he could run faster than anyone present. He was young, and the constant running and work on his family's farm had made him swift. He was confident in his ability.

Útgarða-Loki called forward someone named Hugi to race against Þjálfi. They went outside to a good racing ground. The first race began, and Hugi won, but not by an enormous margin. Útgarða-Loki suggested they race again, giving Þjálfi a chance to redeem himself.

The second race went worse. Hugi won more easily this time, finishing well ahead. For the third race, Þjálfi ran as fast as he possibly could, pushing himself to his absolute limit. Hugi reached the end, turned around, and met Þjálfi before he was even halfway done. The gap between them was so large that Þjálfi had to acknowledge defeat.

Now it was Thor's turn. He claimed he could drink more than anyone present. He had seen the giants drinking during the evening, and he was confident that his capacity for mead exceeded theirs.

Útgarða-Loki had a drinking horn brought out. It looked long but not impossibly so. Útgarða-Loki explained that in his hall, good drinkers could empty this horn in one draught. Most men needed two. But even the weakest drinkers they had ever had could finish it in three drinks. Surely the mighty Thor could manage at least that much.

Thor looked at the horn, judged it manageable, and drank long and deep, his throat working steadily until his breath ran out. He expected to have drained it completely, but when he lowered it, the level had barely changed.

Surprised but not defeated, he drank again, longer this time, until black spots appeared in his vision and his lungs burned for air. The level had dropped noticeably, but the horn was still nearly full, perhaps an inch or two lower than before.

On the third attempt, Thor drank until he thought he would burst, longer than he had ever drunk from any vessel. When he finally stopped, gasping, the level had dropped significantly. But the horn was still more than half full.

Thor gave up, embarrassed and confused. He had drunk enough to fill his stomach painfully, yet he had barely made a dent in this horn. Something was wrong, but he could not figure out what.

Útgarða-Loki suggested a simpler test: lifting his cat. An old gray cat wandered into the hall at just that moment, as if summoned. It looked like an ordinary cat, perhaps elderly and certainly nothing imposing. Thor was asked to lift this cat off the ground completely. After failing at drinking, Thor thought this would be an easy way to redeem himself.

Thor walked over to the cat, bent down, and grabbed it around the middle. He pulled upward, expecting to lift it easily. But the cat arched its back. Thor used more strength. The cat arched higher, its spine bending impossibly far. Thor gritted his teeth and pulled with force enough to lift boulders and uproot trees. The cat's back bent in ways no normal cat's spine could bend. Finally, after straining and sweating, he managed to get one of the cat's four paws off the ground. Just one. The other three paws remained planted firmly on the floor. He stopped, exhausted and humiliated.

Útgarða-Loki observed that the cat was rather large and Thor was rather small, so perhaps this result was not surprising. He offered one final challenge: wrestling. He said he would call forward his old nurse, Elli, for Thor to wrestle. After all, Thor had proven he could not beat a cat, so perhaps an elderly woman would be more his level.

An ancient, withered woman hobbled into the hall. She looked frail and bent with age. She was hardly capable of standing upright, much less wrestling. Thor was insulted by the suggestion that he should wrestle someone so old and weak. It would be shameful to fight an elderly woman, and more shameful still if he lost.

But Útgarða-Loki insisted, suggesting that Thor might be too afraid to accept even this challenge. Thor's pride would not allow that, so he agreed to wrestle Elli.

They grappled. Thor tried to be somewhat gentle at first, not wanting to harm an old woman. But Elli stood firm against his pushes. He began to wrestle more seriously, using real force. Elli pushed back.

The harder Thor fought, the stronger Elli seemed to become. His attempts to throw her failed completely. She simply stood against him, immovable and growing increasingly aggressive. Then she began pushing Thor back. He resisted, but gradually, she forced him backward and downward.

Thor ended up on one knee, forced down by an elderly woman he should have been able to lift with one hand. Útgarða-Loki stopped the match at that point, saying they had seen enough. He declared that there was clearly no point in anyone else in the hall challenging Thor since he had proven unable to beat even Elli in wrestling.

Útgarða-Loki declared that Thor and his companions had failed the contests. He offered them lodging for the night, but the tests were over.

The next morning, Útgarða-Loki escorted them away from the hall. When they were some distance away, he stopped and revealed the truth.

Everything had been illusions. Skrýmir had been Útgarða-Loki in disguise. The food sack with impossible knots had been enchanted. When Thor struck Skrýmir with Mjölnir, Útgarða-Loki had used magic to shift a mountain between himself and the hammer. Thor's three blows had created three valleys in the mountain, striking with enough force to reshape the landscape but never touching the giant himself.

The contests in the hall had also been tricks. Logi was actually wildfire, which consumes everything in its path. No one could out-eat literal fire. Hugi was thought, and nothing moves faster than thought. The drinking horn's other end was in the ocean, so Thor had been drinking the sea. He had lowered the ocean level noticeably; later tradition would associate this with the creation of tides. The cat had been Jörmungandr in disguise, meaning Thor had lifted the World Serpent nearly off the ocean floor. Elli was old age itself, and no one, not even Thor, could defeat time.

Útgarða-Loki said that he would never allow Thor into his hall again, and if he could manage it, Thor would never find the hall again either. Thor raised Mjölnir to strike Útgarða-Loki, but the giant vanished. Thor turned to destroy the hall, but it, too, had disappeared. They stood in an empty plain. The entire experience had been a combination of real magic and clever illusions.

Thor and his companions returned to Asgard.

Thor's Journey to Geirröðr

Thor's visit to the giant Geirröðr was one of the few times he walked into a trap without his usual weapons. Only magic gifts from an unlikely ally saved him. The story began with Loki's capture.

Loki had borrowed Freyja's falcon cloak and was flying over Jötunheim when he flew too close to Geirröðr's hall. The giant spotted him and ordered his servants to capture the bird.

Loki flew to the top of the hall and perched there, thinking he was safely out of reach. He wanted to watch the servants struggle to climb up to him before he flew away. But he waited too long. A servant climbed the wall and grabbed him before he could escape.

They brought the falcon to Geirröðr. The giant looked into its eyes and knew immediately this was not a normal bird. It had intelligence and awareness. This was someone in disguise. Geirröðr demanded that it reveal itself.

However, Loki refused to transform or speak. So, Geirröðr locked him in a chest without food or water for three months.

After three months, Geirröðr opened the chest. Loki was desperate and starving. He was ready to agree to anything. Geirröðr made him an offer. Loki could go free if he brought Thor to Geirröðr's hall without Mjölnir or his belt of strength.

Loki agreed. What choice did he have?

He swore an oath to the giant and returned to Asgard. Somehow, he managed to convince Thor to visit Geirröðr. Loki described the giant's magnificent hall and suggested Thor should see it for himself. As a condition, Loki said Thor should come without his hammer and belt, perhaps as a gesture of goodwill or maybe to prove he did not need them. However Loki framed it, Thor agreed.

They traveled to Jötunheim. On the way, they stopped at the home of a giantess named Gríðr. She was one of Odin's many lovers and had borne him a son named Víðarr. She welcomed Thor but warned him that Geirröðr was dangerous and cunning. Thor was walking into a trap.

Gríðr gave him three items: her own staff, called Gríðarvölr; a pair of iron gloves; and a belt of strength to replace the one he had left behind. With these, she said, he might survive.

Thor and Loki continued to Geirröðr's hall. They had to cross a river called Vimur. As Thor waded across, the water began rising. It rose higher and higher, threatening to sweep them away in a flood.

Thor looked upstream and saw one of Geirröðr's daughters, Gjálp, standing with her legs spread across the river, urinating into it to create the flood. Thor grabbed a boulder and threw it at her. The boulder struck Gjálp, and she fled. The flood subsided.

Thor grabbed a rowan tree growing by the riverbank and pulled himself out of the water. (This is why the rowan tree is called "Thor's salvation.")

Eventually, Loki and Thor reached Geirröðr's hall. Thor was shown to a goat shed to sleep for the night, which was an insult. A guest should not be housed in a shed reserved for animals.

During the night, Thor sat on a chair in the shed. Suddenly, the chair lifted off the ground, rising toward the rafters. Someone—or something—was beneath it, pushing it up to crush Thor against the roof beams.

Thor grabbed Gríðr's staff and pressed the staff against the rafters, forcing the chair back down. There was a terrible cracking sound, followed by screams.

When Thor stood up, he discovered he had broken the backs of Geirröðr's two daughters, Gjálp and Greip. They had been hiding under the chair, trying to crush him.

The next morning, Geirröðr summoned Thor to the main hall. The giant was sitting by a fire in the center of the hall. When Thor entered, Geirröðr picked up a lump of molten iron from the forge with a pair of tongs and hurled it at him.

Thor was wearing Gríðr's iron gloves. He caught the molten iron in midflight. Geirröðr, frightened, dove behind an iron pillar to protect himself.

Thor threw the molten iron back. It passed through the pillar, through Geirröðr's body, through the wall, and into the ground outside.

Geirröðr fell dead. Thor had survived the trap.

The story shows that even Thor could be tricked into danger when separated from his most powerful weapons, but he could still survive through strength, quick thinking, and help from unexpected allies. Without Gríðr's gifts, the outcome likely would have been very different.

Thor's Duel with Hrungnir

Thor's fight with the giant Hrungnir began with a horse race and ended with a stone lodged permanently in Thor's head.

Odin was riding through Jötunheim on Sleipnir when he encountered a giant named Hrungnir. Hrungnir admired Sleipnir and boasted that his own horse, Gullfaxi ("Golden Mane"), was faster. Odin, never one to turn down such a challenge, bet his head that no horse in Jötunheim could outrun Sleipnir.

The race began. Odin galloped ahead on Sleipnir, and Hrungnir chased after him on Gullfaxi. The giant was so focused on catching Odin that he did not notice where they were going until he had already ridden through the gates of Asgard itself.

The gods could not simply kill Hrungnir inside Asgard. He was their guest now, even uninvited. So, they invited him to drink with them.

Hrungnir drank heavily. The more he drank, the more boastful he became. He announced he would pick up all of Valhalla and carry it back to Jötunheim. He would sink Asgard beneath the ocean. He would kill all the gods except Freyja and Sif, whom he would take home with him.

The gods tolerated this because he was their guest, but they were growing tired of his boasts and insults. But Hrungnir kept drinking and bragging. Finally, the gods called for Thor.

Thor arrived at Valhalla and saw a giant sitting at the gods' feast, drinking from Freyja's cup and making threats. Thor raised Mjölnir, ready to kill Hrungnir immediately.

But before he could strike, Hrungnir pointed out that killing an unarmed guest would bring Thor no honor. If Thor wanted to fight him, they should meet in proper combat at the border between their realms. Hrungnir would bring his weapons. Thor could bring his hammer. They would fight, and whoever won would earn legitimate glory.

Thor agreed. They would meet at the border of Jötunheim, a location called Grjótúnagarðar ("Stone-Yard Enclosure").

The giants, hearing about this combat, became worried. Hrungnir was one of their strongest, but Thor had killed countless giants. They needed to give him every possible advantage.

They built a helper for him—a giant made entirely of clay, nine leagues tall, with a mare's heart inside it. They could not find a heart large enough among the giants, so they had to use a horse's heart. They called this clay giant Mökkurkalfi ("Mist-Calf" or "Cloud-Calf").

Hrungnir alone was formidable. He had a heart made of hard stone. It was pointed and three-cornered. His head was also stone. He carried a stone shield and a massive whetstone as his weapon. When the day came, Hrungnir stood with his shield in front of him and his whetstone on his shoulder, with Mökkurkalfi standing beside him.

Thor arrived with Þjálfi. The servant had a plan. He ran ahead to Hrungnir and told him that Thor was approaching from underground, planning to attack from below. Hrungnir, believing this, put his shield beneath his feet and stood on it, holding his whetstone ready.

Then Thor appeared before him with thunder and lightning. He raised Mjölnir and hurled it at Hrungnir.

Hrungnir threw his whetstone to meet the hammer.

The two weapons collided in midair. The whetstone shattered. One piece fell to earth and became the origin of all whetstones in the world. Another piece flew toward Thor and struck him in the forehead, embedding itself in his skull. Thor fell to the ground.

But Mjölnir continued forward after breaking the whetstone. It struck Hrungnir's head and smashed his stone skull into fragments. The giant fell dead, and as he fell, one of his massive legs landed across Thor's neck, pinning him to the ground.

Meanwhile, Þjálfi fought Mökkurkalfi. The clay giant was huge but clumsy, and it had only a horse's heart to animate it. Þjálfi killed it easily. It fell apart when struck, wet clay collapsing into mud.

However, Thor was still pinned beneath Hrungnir's leg. All the gods tried to lift it off him. None of them could move the giant's leg enough to free Thor.

Then Thor's son Magni arrived. He was only three nights old, but he was already enormously strong. Magni grabbed Hrungnir's leg and lifted it off his father without any real effort.

Thor stood up, the whetstone still embedded in his forehead. He thanked Magni and gave him Gullfaxi, Hrungnir's horse, as a reward for saving his life.

Odin was displeased by this. He thought Gullfaxi should have gone to him. After all, he had won the horse from Hrungnir in their race. Giving it to Magni seemed like a waste.

The whetstone remained a problem. It was lodged in Thor's skull, and no one could remove it. They brought a völva (seeress) named Gróa to see if her magic could draw it out. She began chanting spells over Thor, singing galdr that should loosen the stone fragment.

Thor, feeling the stone beginning to shift, was so grateful that he wanted to reward Gróa. He told her that he had recently been in Jötunheim and had met her husband, Aurvandil. He had carried Aurvandil across icy rivers in a basket, and one of Aurvandil's toes had stuck out of the basket and frozen. Thor broke off the frozen toe and threw it into the sky, where it became a star. Aurvandil was fine otherwise and would be coming home soon.

Gróa was so excited by this news that her husband was alive and coming home that she forgot the spell she was chanting. The whetstone stopped moving. It remained lodged in Thor's skull forever.

The stone became a reminder not to throw whetstones across a room because disturbing a whetstone might jar the fragment in Thor's head and cause him pain.

The Theft of Thor's Hammer

Thor woke up one morning, and his hammer was gone.

This was a catastrophe. Mjölnir was Thor's primary weapon. He used it to defend both Asgard and Midgard against giants. Without it, Thor was still strong, but he could not protect the ordered worlds from the threats that constantly pressed against them. Whoever had stolen Mjölnir had struck at the heart of the gods' security.

Thor told Loki immediately. Despite their complicated relationship, Loki was the person the gods called when they needed something found or when they needed to deal with tricky situations. Loki went to Freyja and borrowed her falcon cloak, which allowed the wearer to fly. He transformed into a falcon and flew to Jötunheim to search for information.

He found the giant Þrymr sitting on a burial mound, braiding gold leashes for his dogs and trimming the manes of his horses. Þrymr was clearly in a good mood, which suggested he knew something. Loki asked whether he knew anything about Thor's missing hammer.

Þrymr admitted that he had stolen Mjölnir. He had hidden it eight leagues under the earth, where no one would find it. He would return the hammer on one condition: the gods had to give him Freyja as his wife.

This was an outrageous demand. Freyja was one of the most powerful goddesses, a practitioner of seiðr magic, and not someone who could be traded away like property. But Þrymr was serious, and without Mjölnir, the gods were vulnerable.

Loki flew back to Asgard and reported what Þrymr had said. The gods held a council to discuss what to do. Loki went to Freyja and suggested she put on a bridal veil and prepare for the journey to Jötunheim.

Freyja was furious. She was so angry that her necklace, Brísingamen, shook loose and fell. She refused. She would not marry a giant. She would not be given away as payment for Thor's hammer.

The gods debated alternatives. The problem was that they could not attack Jötunheim without Thor's hammer. They could not negotiate for better terms because Þrymr held all the leverage. They needed Mjölnir back, but they could not give Þrymr what he demanded.

Heimdall, the watchman of the gods, proposed a solution that was both clever and humiliating. Thor should dress as Freyja and go to Jötunheim as the bride. Loki would accompany him, disguised as a bridesmaid. They would infiltrate Þrymr's hall, get close to Mjölnir, and Thor could reclaim his hammer once it was within reach.

Thor hated this idea. Dress as a woman? Pretend to be a bride? Every masculine instinct in Thor's nature rebelled against the suggestion. He argued that the other gods would mock him forever if he dressed in women's clothing.

Loki pointed out that without Mjölnir, the giants would invade Asgard. They would conquer the realm of the gods. Thor could either accept temporary humiliation or watch everything he had sworn to protect be destroyed.

Thor reluctantly agreed. The goddesses dressed him in a bridal gown with a veil to hide his face. They placed Brísingamen around his neck, and they added bridal linens and women's jewelry. Loki dressed as a bridesmaid, and together, they got into Thor's goat-drawn chariot to ride to Jötunheim.

They arrived at Þrymr's hall. The giant was delighted that the gods actually decided to give him Freyja. He ordered a feast prepared to celebrate the wedding. The hall filled with giants, all there to witness Þrymr marrying one of the most beautiful and powerful beings in all the Nine Worlds.

Thor dressed as Freyja.[12]

At the feast, problems immediately became apparent. "Freyja" ate an entire ox. Then eight salmon. Then all the delicacies meant for the female guests. "She" washed it down with three casks of mead. Þrymr was astonished—he had never seen a bride eat so much.

Loki, thinking quickly, explained that Freyja had been so excited about the wedding that she had not eaten for eight days and nights. She was simply making up for lost time. Þrymr accepted this explanation.

At one point, Þrymr tried to kiss his bride and lifted the veil. He saw Thor's eyes, burning, furious eyes that looked nothing like Freyja's, and jumped back in terror. Loki explained that Freyja had not slept for eight nights in her anticipation of the wedding, which was why her eyes looked so fierce.

Þrymr was convinced, or at least willing to proceed. He ordered that Mjölnir be brought forth and laid on the bride's lap to consecrate the marriage, following the traditional use of Thor's hammer to bless weddings.

This was the moment they had been waiting for. As soon as Mjölnir touched Thor's lap, he grabbed it, immediately throwing off the veil. He roared with both rage and relief at having his hammer back and began killing every giant in the hall.

He killed Þrymr first, smashing the giant's skull in. Then he killed Þrymr's sister, who had asked for wedding gifts. Then he killed all the other giants who had been celebrating the wedding. Thor went through the hall like a storm, Mjölnir rising and falling, until every giant in Þrymr's hall was dead.

They left Jötunheim with Mjölnir recovered and Thor's pride somewhat restored. Yes, he had dressed as a bride and infiltrated a giant's wedding feast. Yes, other gods would know about it and probably never let him forget. But he had his hammer back, the threat was ended, and Freyja had not been forced into an unwanted marriage.

This story became popular in Viking culture, appearing in multiple sources and even depicted in stone carvings. Part of its appeal was seeing Thor in such an unusual situation, relying on deception rather than direct force. The story also showed Freyja's refusal to accept being traded away and that giants could be clever and dangerous in ways beyond physical threats. Þrymr had found the one thing he could steal that would give him leverage over the gods, and only through trickery, using Loki's methods rather than Thor's usual approach, could the gods recover what had been taken.

Loki Steals Brísingamen

Freyja's necklace, Brísingamen, was breathtakingly beautiful. She had acquired it by spending one night with each of the four dwarves who forged it. From the moment she received it, she wore it constantly.

The story of how Loki stole the necklace comes primarily from a late source called *Sörla þáttr eða Heðins saga ok Högna*, a 14th- or 15th-century text written long after Iceland's conversion to Christianity. The tale is heavily moralistic in tone, framing Freyja's acquisition of the necklace as sexual misconduct requiring punishment. This Christian interpretation would not necessarily have been part of the original pagan myth. Despite its late date and moral framing, *Sörla þáttr* preserves details about the theft that do not appear in the earlier Eddas.

According to this later version, Odin learned how Freyja had obtained Brísingamen. Whether he discovered it through his ravens, through his wanderings, or through some other means, the text does not specify. Regardless of how he found out, Odin was displeased, and he decided Freyja needed to be taught a lesson.

So, Odin summoned Loki and gave him a task. He had to steal Brísingamen from Freyja.

Loki traveled to Freyja's hall, Sessrúmnir in Fólkvangr. He found every door locked and every window sealed. He circled the building looking for an entrance and discovered that the hall was completely secure. Not even a mouse could squeeze through the gaps in the walls.

But Loki was nothing if not persistent. He kept searching until he found one tiny opening near the gables—a hole so small that only an insect could fit through it. Loki transformed himself into a fly and crawled through the gap.

Inside Sessrúmnir, Freyja lay asleep in her bed. She was wearing Brísingamen. The necklace's clasp was at the back of her neck, pressed against her pillow, where Loki could not reach it without disturbing her.

Loki transformed into a flea. He landed on Freyja's cheek and bit down hard. She stirred in her sleep and rolled slightly to one side. The movement was enough. The clasp was now accessible.

Loki resumed his normal form, reached out carefully, and undid the clasp. He slipped Brísingamen off Freyja's neck without waking her. Then he transformed back into a fly and escaped through the same tiny gap he had used to enter.

When Freyja woke and found the necklace gone, her rage was absolute. She knew who had taken it. Only Loki would dare such a theft, and only Odin would have sent him. She went directly to Odin and demanded that he return Brísingamen.

Odin agreed, but he set a price for its return. Freyja would have to cause strife between two powerful kings, Högni and Heðinn. She would have to use her magic to ensure they fought an eternal battle. Every day, they would kill each other and all their warriors, and every night, everyone would be resurrected to fight the following morning again. This war would continue forever unless someone powerful enough intervened to stop it.

Freyja had no choice. She agreed to Odin's terms. She worked her magic and caused the never-ending war between the two kings. Odin returned Brísingamen to her.

As mentioned, this elaborate version of events appears only in *Sörla þáttr*. The earlier sources tell a much simpler story. A fragmentary poem called *Húsdrápa*, preserved in pieces in Snorri's *Prose Edda*, mentions the theft of Brísingamen and a fight between Heimdall and Loki over its possession. According to *Húsdrápa*, the two gods battled at a place called Singasteinn. Both transformed into seals during the fight. Heimdall won the contest and recovered the necklace, returning it to Freyja. That is all the earlier source preserves. There are no details about how the theft occurred and no mention of Odin's involvement or eternal wars.

The two versions may represent different traditions about the same event, or they may be entirely separate incidents, with the *Húsdrápa* describing one theft and recovery and the *Sörla þáttr* describing another. What both versions agree on is that there was a theft of the necklace.

At Ragnarök, Heimdall and Loki would meet on the battlefield and kill each other. Whether their final confrontation had anything to do with this earlier conflict over the necklace, the sources do not explicitly say. But the two gods clearly had history.

Otter's Ransom and the Cursed Gold

This story comes from *Skáldskaparmál* in Snorri's *Prose Edda* and the *Völsunga Saga*, a 13th-century prose work that expands on earlier poetic material. It connects the gods to the cursed treasure that would eventually destroy the Völsung dynasty, and it shows Loki solving one problem by creating another—a pattern that defined much of his existence.

Odin, Loki, and Hœnir were traveling together through Midgard. They came to a waterfall where they saw an otter catching salmon. The otter had caught a large fish and was eating it on the riverbank, completely absorbed in its meal.

Loki picked up a stone and threw it at the otter. His aim was perfect. The stone killed the otter instantly. Loki was pleased that he had killed the otter, as they could eat the salmon it had been feasting on.

The three gods skinned the otter and carried the pelt and the salmon to a nearby home, asking for hospitality for the night. The dwarf who owned it was named Hreiðmarr. He had three sons called Fáfnir, Regin, and Ótr.

When Hreiðmarr saw the otter pelt, his face went pale. The otter that Loki had killed was his son Ótr, who could shapeshift into otter form and often hunted fish in the river in that shape.

Hreiðmarr called his two remaining sons. Together, they seized the three gods and bound them. Hreiðmarr demanded compensation for his son's death. This was known as wergild, the traditional payment owed when someone killed another person's family member.

He said they must fill the otter skin with gold and then cover it completely with more gold on the outside. Every hair of the pelt must be hidden beneath gold, or the debt would not be paid.

The gods agreed. They did not really have a choice; they were bound and at Hreiðmarr's mercy. But they did not have that much gold with them. They sent Loki to acquire it, while Odin and Hœnir remained as hostages.

Loki knew where to find gold. He went to the goddess Rán and borrowed her net—the same net she used to catch drowning sailors. Then he traveled to a waterfall where a dwarf named Andvari lived in the form of a pike, guarding a treasure hoard.

Loki caught Andvari in Rán's net. The dwarf begged to be released. Loki demanded all of Andvari's gold as ransom for his life.

Andvari brought out his treasure—a massive hoard of gold that he had accumulated over the ages. Loki took it all. But as he was leaving, he noticed Andvari trying to hide a small ring on his finger.

Loki demanded that ring too. Andvari pleaded to keep it. The ring was called Andvaranaut, and it had the power to generate more gold. With it, he could rebuild his hoard. Without it, he would have nothing.

Loki took the ring anyway.

Andvari, upset at losing this priceless treasure, cursed it. He spoke words of power over Andvaranaut, declaring that the ring and all the gold it created would bring death to everyone who possessed it. The treasure would destroy whoever owned it, passing from hand to hand through murder and betrayal until it drowned in blood.

Loki ignored the curse and brought the gold back to Hreiðmarr's farm. They stuffed the otter skin with gold until it was full. Then they piled gold on top of it, covering every hair of the pelt.

When they were done, Hreiðmarr examined the pelt carefully. He found one whisker still visible. The pelt was not completely covered. The debt was not yet paid.

Loki had one piece of gold left—Andvaranaut, the cursed ring. He placed it on the exposed whisker, covering it completely.

Now, the debt was paid. Odin, Loki, and Hœnir were released and left immediately.

But before they could get far, Loki called back to Hreiðmarr to tell him about Andvari's curse. The gold would bring death to whoever possessed it, Loki said. It seemed that he wanted Hreiðmarr to know exactly what he had demanded as payment for his son.

The curse proved true. Fáfnir killed his father Hreiðmarr to claim the gold. Then Fáfnir transformed himself into a dragon and lay on top of the treasure hoard, guarding it obsessively, breathing poison to prevent anyone from getting near it. He became a monster defined entirely by his desire to possess the cursed gold.

Regin survived by fleeing. He would later raise a hero named Sigurd and send him to kill Fáfnir and claim the treasure. That treasure— Andvari's cursed gold, paid as an otter's ransom—would pass through the Völsung dynasty, bringing death and destruction to everyone who touched it, exactly as the dwarf had promised.

The Mead of Poetry

The Mead of Poetry was the most precious substance in the Nine Worlds for anyone who cared about words, knowledge, or artistic expression. Anyone who drank it would become a skilled poet and scholar, able to compose verses of great beauty and speak with wisdom. The story of how this mead was created and how Odin stole it involves murder, betrayal, and giant-slaying.

It began with Kvasir, the being created from the combined spit of all the gods after the Æsir-Vanir War. Kvasir traveled the worlds, and the sources tell us he shared knowledge with those who asked. His wisdom was absolute. There was no question he could not answer, no problem he could not solve.

Two dwarves, Fjalar and Galar, invited Kvasir to their home for a private conversation. Instead of talking, they killed Kvasir, drained his blood into three containers—two vats called Són and Boðn and a pot called Óðrerir—and mixed the blood with honey.

The mixture became the Mead of Poetry. Anyone who drank it would gain Kvasir's wisdom and eloquence. The dwarves had transformed the wisest being in existence into a drink.

When the gods asked what had happened to Kvasir, Fjalar and Galar claimed he had choked on his own intelligence. There was no one wise enough to challenge him with questions, so his wisdom had suffocated him. The gods accepted this unlikely explanation, possibly because they had no proof of murder and could not act without evidence.

Fjalar and Galar did not enjoy the mead. Instead, they committed more murders. They invited a giant named Gilling and his wife to visit them. They took Gilling out on a boat and rowed to a spot where they knew there were rocks just below the surface. They then capsized the boat deliberately. Gilling, who could not swim, drowned. The dwarves rowed back to shore.

When Gilling's wife learned her husband was dead, she wept loudly. Fjalar, annoyed by her crying, offered to take her to the spot where Gilling had drowned so she could mourn properly. When she walked through the doorway of their hall, Galar dropped a millstone on her head from above, killing her.

These murders had consequences. Gilling's son, Suttungr, came to investigate his parents' deaths. Realizing the dwarves were behind them, he seized the two and carried them out to a skerry—a small rocky island—that would be covered by the ocean at high tide. The dwarves would drown when the tide came in. Suttungr was satisfied with this method of execution.

Fjalar and Galar pleaded for their lives. They offered Suttungr the Mead of Poetry as compensation for his parents' deaths. After thinking on it, Suttungr agreed. He took the mead, released the dwarves, and brought the precious liquid back to his home in the mountains.

Suttungr hid the mead inside a mountain called Hnitbjörg. He placed it in a chamber deep within it and told his daughter Gunnlöð to guard it. She would sit in the mountain with the mead, allowing no one to enter or drink it.

This was where things stood when Odin learned about the mead's existence. The All-Father wanted it. The Mead of Poetry contained the wisdom of Kvasir, distilled and preserved. For Odin, who sacrificed an eye and hanged himself for knowledge, the mead was irresistible.

Odin disguised himself as a wanderer called Bölverkr, meaning "Evil-Doer" or "Evil-Worker," and traveled to the lands near Suttungr's mountain. He found nine servants working in a field, mowing hay with scythes. They belonged to Suttungr's brother Baugi, who owned the land and employed these men. Odin approached them and offered to sharpen their scythes with his whetstone.

The men accepted, as their scythes had grown dull from the hard work. A good sharpening would make the rest of the day much easier. So, Odin took out his whetstone and worked on each scythe in turn. His sharpening was so effective, his technique so skilled, that the scythes became sharper than they had ever been before. The men marveled at how easily the blades cut through grass and stems.

Odin asked whether they wanted to buy his whetstone. All nine men said yes immediately. With a whetstone this good, they could keep their tools sharp, and their work would go much faster.

Odin tossed the whetstone into the air. The nine men scrambled to catch it, pushing and shoving each other, reaching desperately for the falling stone. In the confusion and violence of their competition, and with the sharp scythes in their hands, the men wounded each other fatally. All nine ended up dead or dying in the field.

Odin watched this happen and then went to Baugi's home. He presented himself as a wanderer called Bölverkr and noticed that Baugi had lost his workers. Odin offered to do the work of all nine men throughout the summer, to be paid only when the work was done.

Baugi agreed, and they negotiated terms. When Odin was asked what payment he wanted, he said he wanted one drink of the Mead of Poetry that Baugi's brother Suttungr possessed. Baugi replied that he did not control the mead; his brother Suttungr guarded it jealously and refused to share even a drop with anyone. But if Bölverkr worked all summer and completed the work of nine men, Baugi would accompany him to

Suttungr and help him try to get that drink.

Odin worked all summer, somehow accomplishing the labor of nine men by himself. Whether through magic, extraordinary endurance, or simply working every hour, he completed everything the nine dead men would have done. The fields were mowed, and the hay was gathered. Baugi had no grounds to complain about the quality or quantity of his work.

When summer ended and the work was complete, Baugi and Odin went together to Suttungr's hall. Baugi explained that Bölverkr had worked as nine men all summer and that the agreed payment was one drink of the Mead of Poetry. Would Suttungr allow this?

Suttungr refused. Not a single drop of the mead would be given to anyone, regardless of what work they had done or what Baugi had promised. Suttungr had paid for the mead with the lives of Fjalar and Galar in a sense—he had spared them after threatening to drown them. He had hidden it in a mountain and had set his daughter to guard it. No stranger would drink even a sip.

Baugi and Odin left Suttungr's hall. Outside, Odin revealed to Baugi that they would need to use deception and force rather than negotiation. He produced an auger—a drill for boring through stone—called Rati. This was no ordinary tool but something made specifically for penetrating rock. Odin asked Baugi to drill through the mountain to the chamber where Gunnlöð guarded the mead.

Baugi began drilling. He worked at the mountain's base, boring into solid stone, working the auger deeper and deeper. After much labor, he stopped and claimed he had drilled all the way through to the chamber. Odin tested this by blowing into the hole Baugi had made. Stone chips and dust blew back into Odin's face. Baugi was lying; he had not drilled through completely, and the hole was still blocked.

Odin told Baugi to keep drilling. Perhaps Baugi had genuinely thought he was through, or perhaps he was trying to help his brother by preventing access to the mead. Either way, he continued working the auger. Finally, after more drilling, he told Odin to test again. This time, when Odin blew into the hole, air passed through freely into the chamber beyond. The auger had broken through.

Odin transformed himself into a snake and began slithering through the hole. Baugi, either trying to protect his brother's treasure or angry at being tricked into helping this theft, grabbed the auger and stabbed at the snake as it crawled. But Odin was already through the hole, his tail disappearing into the mountain just as Baugi's thrust came down. Baugi had failed to stop him.

Inside the mountain chamber, Odin found Gunnlöð sitting alone with the three containers of mead: Óðrerir, Boðn, and Són. She had been in this chamber for a long time, sitting in isolation with only the precious liquid for company.

Odin spent three nights with her. In exchange for these three nights, Gunnlöð agreed to let Odin take three drinks of the mead.

Odin drank from Óðrerir, the pot that contained what was likely the purest or most powerful portion of the mead. He did not sip. He drank the entire container in one draught, emptying it completely. Then he turned to Boðn, one of the vats, and drank that entirely as well. Then he drained Són, the other vat. Before Gunnlöð could say anything, Odin transformed into an eagle and flew toward the hole he had entered through.

Suttungr discovered the theft immediately. He transformed into an eagle and pursued Odin, flying in rage at the theft of his treasure and the deception of his daughter.

The gods in Asgard saw two eagles approaching, one fleeing and one pursuing. They set out containers in the courtyard. Odin flew over Asgard and spat out the mead into the containers, emptying his stomach as quickly as possible to preserve what he had stolen.

But Suttungr was close behind, and in his haste, Odin lost some of the mead. Some of it fell outside Asgard's walls. The gods did not bother collecting this portion.

The sources explain that this is why there are two kinds of poets. Those who drink from the portion Odin saved are true poets with genuine skill and inspiration. Those who drink from the portion that fell randomly are bad poets—people who write terrible verses despite thinking they have talent.

Odin kept the saved mead in Asgard, sharing it with the gods and with humans he favored. To receive the Mead of Poetry from Odin was to be marked as a poet of great skill, someone whose verses would be remembered.

The Building of Asgard's Wall

Shortly after the Æsir-Vanir War ended, Asgard faced a serious security problem. The war had damaged the realm's defenses, and the walls that protected Asgard from giants and other threats had been broken or were insufficient. The gods needed fortifications strong enough to keep out any enemy, walls that could withstand assault from the most powerful giants. The problem was that building such a wall would take years—perhaps decades—of hard labor, and the gods had many other demands to attend to. They could not spare the resources to build adequate defenses themselves.

A builder appeared at Asgard's gates and offered a solution. He appeared to be a large and strong man. He was also clearly confident. He claimed he could build a wall around Asgard that would be impregnable. No giant would ever breach it. No enemy could break through. Asgard would be completely protected.

The gods were interested but also suspicious. Who was this stranger offering to do what should be impossible? What were his true motivations? And most importantly, what payment would he demand for such work? They asked him to name his price.

The builder said he wanted the sun, the moon, and Freyja as his wife.

The gods were horrified. Taking the sun and moon would plunge all the worlds into eternal darkness and freezing cold, ending life as effectively as Ragnarök would. And Freyja, one of the most powerful goddesses, could not be traded away like property.

The gods told the builder his price was too high. They could not agree to such terms. The builder should leave, and they would find another way to protect Asgard.

However, Loki intervened in the gods' private discussions. He pointed out that the builder was asking for an impossible payment, but he was also promising to do impossible work. He claimed he could build a massive wall around all of Asgard single-handedly in a reasonable time frame. That was clearly impossible. No one could do that much work that quickly.

Loki's suggestion was clever. He told the gods they should set conditions so strict that the builder would inevitably fail. They could agree to his outrageous price, but only if he met impossible deadlines and restrictions. The builder would then work, build as much as he could, but ultimately fail to complete the wall in time. The gods would get a partially built wall for free when the builder failed to meet the conditions, and they would not have to pay anything.

The gods debated Loki's proposal. It was risky. What if the builder somehow succeeded? But Loki argued persuasively that the conditions they set would make success impossible. The potential gain seemed worth the minimal risk.

They called the builder back with a counteroffer. He could have what he asked for, but only under very specific conditions. First, he had to complete the entire wall in a single winter, before the first day of summer. Not just most of the wall, not just the major sections, but every stone in place, the entire fortification complete and functional. Second, he had to work entirely alone. No other giants could help him. He could have no laborers, no assistants, no one. He would build the entire wall by himself in one winter, or he would receive nothing.

The builder considered these terms. They were harsh, probably impossible. He said he would agree, but only if he could have his horse, Svaðilfari, to help haul stones and materials. Just the horse, no other assistance.

The gods debated this. Loki argued that a horse did not count as "someone" helping. It was just an animal, a tool like a cart or a sled. The builder was still working alone—one person and one horse could not possibly complete such massive construction in one winter. Loki believed the gods should agree to the builder's terms because it did not actually change the impossibility of the task.

And so the gods accepted. The builder could use his horse, Svaðilfari, but no other help of any kind. And the deadline was firm: every stone had to be in place by the first day of summer. If even a single stone was not placed, if any part of the wall remained incomplete, he would receive no payment whatsoever.

The work began on the first day of winter. The builder and his horse, Svaðilfari, started immediately, and what the gods saw shocked them. Svaðilfari was not a normal horse. It was extraordinarily strong, capable of hauling stones that should have required teams of oxen or dozens of normal horses. The stallion pulled massive blocks of stone as if they weighed nothing, working tirelessly from dawn until well after dark.

And the builder himself was incredibly skilled. He knew exactly where to place each stone, how to fit them together, and how to build walls that would stand for ages. He worked with speed and precision that seemed impossible for one person. Each day, more of the wall went up. Each week, significant progress was visible.

The gods watched with growing concern. This was not supposed to be possible. The builder was actually making real progress at a pace they had not anticipated. As winter continued, the wall grew higher and longer. The builder was on schedule—or even ahead of schedule.

The gods called an emergency council. Who had advised them to agree to these terms? Who had suggested they could get the work done for free? They turned on Loki, blaming him for the situation. If the builder finished the wall, they would lose the sun, the moon, and Freyja. The consequences would be catastrophic.

They threatened Loki with torture and death unless he found a way to prevent the builder from completing the work. Loki swore he would fix the problem, though he did not say how.

That night, as the builder's horse, Svaðilfari, was hauling the final stones for the gate, a mare appeared from the forest. She whinnied at Svaðilfari, and the stallion immediately became interested in her. The mare ran into the forest. Svaðilfari, overcome by the distraction, broke free from the builder's control and chased after the mare.

The builder spent the entire night trying to catch his horse, but the mare led Svaðilfari on a chase that lasted until dawn. By the time the builder got his horse back, night had passed. The first day of summer had arrived, and the gate was not complete. The builder had failed to meet the deadline.

The builder was furious. In his rage, he dropped his disguise and revealed his true giant nature. The gods realized they had been dealing with a particularly dangerous jötunn who had been hiding his full size and strength. They called for Thor.

Thor arrived, saw what was happening, and immediately killed the builder with Mjölnir. The giant who had nearly completed Asgard's wall fell dead, and the gods did not have to pay him anything.

Some time later, Loki returned to Asgard, leading an eight-legged foal. This was Sleipnir, the offspring of Svaðilfari and the mare, who had been Loki in disguised form. Whether Loki had planned the pregnancy as part of his solution or whether it was an unexpected consequence of the distraction, the sources do not specify.

Loki gave Sleipnir to Odin, and the eight-legged horse became Odin's mount. Sleipnir could run faster than any other horse, could gallop across sky and sea, and would serve Odin faithfully.

The sources present what had happened without extensive moralizing. The builder had worked and nearly completed the impossible task. The gods prevented his success through trickery and then killed him. The wall stood as both protection and a reminder of this transaction.

Chapter 6: The Fall of the Curtain

The Death of Baldr

Baldr was described as the best of the gods. He was beautiful beyond comparison, wise in judgment, eloquent in speech, and so fair that light radiated from him. His eyelashes were compared to a particularly white flower that was called Baldr's brow; the sources were likely referring to chamomile.

He lived in Breiðablik, meaning "Broad-Gleam," a hall described as being a place where nothing unclean could exist. He was married to Nanna, daughter of Nep, and they had a son named Forseti, who would become a god of justice and mediation.

While Thor was the strongest and Odin was the wisest, Baldr was the best. His death would prove to be the beginning of the end for the gods.

One night, Baldr began having terrible dreams. These were not ordinary dreams but visions that deeply troubled him. They hinted that his life was in danger. He told the other gods, and they took them seriously. Dreams in Norse culture were often prophetic, glimpses of *wyrd* unfolding, and warnings about what was coming.

Baldr's dreams worried everyone in Asgard. If the best of the gods was dreaming of danger, if light itself was troubled by visions of darkness, then something was deeply wrong.

Frigg decided to act. She traveled through all the worlds and extracted oaths from nearly all things in existence not to harm Baldr. Fire, water, metals, stones, earth, trees, diseases, beasts, birds, poisons—all promised not to harm him.

Once everything had sworn these oaths, Baldr became invulnerable. The gods tested this protection. They would have Baldr stand in their assembly while others threw weapons at him without harm. Nothing hurt him. Everything bounced off or missed. The gods made this a regular entertainment at their gatherings.

Loki watched these games. He disguised himself as a woman and visited Frigg at her hall, Fensalir. He struck up a conversation, asking about the games and why everyone was throwing items at Baldr. Frigg explained that everything had sworn oaths not to harm her son.

Loki asked whether absolutely every single thing had sworn. Frigg admitted there was one exception: the mistletoe growing west of Valhalla. It had seemed too young and insignificant to bother with. Everything substantial had sworn, though.

Loki went out and found the mistletoe. He fashioned it into a weapon— a dart or spear or perhaps just a sharpened branch. He brought it back to where the gods were playing their game.

Everyone was throwing things at Baldr except Höðr, Baldr's blind brother, who stood apart, unable to participate. He could not see where Baldr was standing, and he had no weapon to throw.

Loki approached Höðr with false friendliness. He offered to help Höðr join the fun, to guide his hand and provide a weapon—the branch of mistletoe. Höðr agreed, trusting Loki. Loki positioned him, placed the mistletoe in his hand, and guided his throw.

The mistletoe flew true. It struck Baldr and pierced through him.

The laughter stopped. Everything stopped. Baldr fell dead, struck by the only weapon that could kill him, thrown by his own blind brother's hand, guided by Loki's malice.

The gods gathered around Baldr's body.[18]

The *Völuspá* calls this the greatest misfortune ever to befall gods and men, as it was the beginning of all disasters leading to Ragnarök. The gods stood in shocked silence. They were in a sacred space where violence was forbidden, so they were unable to take immediate revenge even though they knew Loki had engineered this murder.

The texts don't actually say why Loki did this. It seems likely that he was jealous of Baldr, as he was the most adored by the gods. But it is possible that it was just in Loki's nature to play tricks. And it is also possible that this was fated to happen, as this was the key event that led to Ragnarök.

Frigg asked whether anyone would ride to Helheim to try to ransom Baldr back. Hermóðr the Bold volunteered. Odin lent him Sleipnir, the eight-legged horse, for the dangerous journey.

Meanwhile, the gods prepared Baldr's funeral. They brought his body to his ship, Hringhorni, described as the greatest of all ships. But when they tried to launch it, even all the gods together could not move it.

They sent to Jötunheim for a giantess named Hyrrokkin. She arrived riding a wolf with vipers for reins. Four berserkers tried to hold her mount and could not control it until they knocked it unconscious. Hyrrokkin pushed the ship with one hand so violently that fire sparked from the wooden rollers and the earth shook. Thor became furious at this display and nearly killed her, but the other gods stopped him.

They placed Baldr's body on the ship, arranging it with his possessions. Nanna stood on the shore watching her husband's funeral preparations. Her heart broke from grief. She died there, overwhelmed by sorrow. They placed her body beside Baldr's on the pyre.

Odin placed his ring, Draupnir, one of his most precious possessions, with Baldr. Thor consecrated the pyre with Mjölnir. A dwarf named Litr ran in front of Thor during the consecration, and Thor kicked him into the fire.

They set the ship aflame and pushed it to sea. The burning ship drifted away. Gods, giants, and beings from all Nine Worlds watched it burn.

While this was happening, Hermóðr was riding to Helheim. He rode for nine nights through dark valleys so deep he could not see anything. He came to the river Gjöll, which marked the boundary between the living world and Hel's realm. A bridge called Gjallarbrú crossed it, covered with gleaming gold.

A maiden named Móðguðr guarded the bridge. She noted that five companies of dead men had ridden over the bridge the day before, but the bridge thundered less under all of them than under Hermóðr alone. He had color in his skin, and he breathed—why was a living man riding toward Hel's realm?

Hermóðr explained he was seeking Baldr. Móðguðr confirmed Baldr had passed and directed him down the road to Hel's realm.

He reached Helheim's enormous gates. Rather than try to open them, he spurred Sleipnir forward, and the eight-legged horse leaped over the gates in a single bound.

Inside, Hermóðr found Baldr sitting in the high seat of honor in Hel's hall. The next morning, he asked Hel to release Baldr, explaining the grief his death had caused and offering whatever ransom she required.

Hel set a condition. If everything in all the worlds wept for Baldr, she would release him. But if even one thing refused to weep, he would remain.

The gods sent messengers everywhere. Everything wept—people, gods, giants, earth, stones, trees, and metals. Moisture appeared on all surfaces as the cosmos mourned.

But the messengers found a giantess named Þökk sitting in a cave. She refused to weep. Because just one being refused, Baldr would remain dead. The gods suspected Þökk was Loki in disguise, his final act to ensure Baldr stayed dead.

Loki fled to the mountains and built a house with four doors to watch for the gods who were sure to pursue him. During the day, he transformed into a salmon and hid in a waterfall. One night, while in his house, he sat making the first fishing net, working out whether such a device could catch a salmon.

Odin spotted him from Hliðskjálf. The gods approached his new home to apprehend him. Loki threw the net in the fire to destroy the evidence and jumped into the waterfall. The gods found the burned net pattern in the ashes. One of the gods recognized what it was, and they copied the design.

They dragged the net through the waterfall multiple times. Finally, as Loki leaped over the net trying to escape, Thor caught the salmon in mid-leap, gripping it so hard near the tail that salmon have been narrow there ever since.

The gods dragged Loki to a cave and captured his sons. They turned one son, Váli, into a wolf, who immediately killed his brother Narfi. They used Narfi's entrails as rope to bind Loki across three stone slabs. The entrails turned to iron chains.

Skaði, whose father Loki had helped to kill, placed a venomous serpent above Loki's head to drip poison on his face. Loki's wife, Sigyn, stayed with him, holding a bowl to catch the venom. When the bowl filled, and she turned to empty it, venom dripped directly onto Loki. His writhing in agony caused earthquakes.

And there Loki would remain, bound and tortured, until Ragnarök freed him for the final battle.

Sigyn holding the bowl above Loki's head.[14]

Fimbulwinter: The Beginning of the End

The approach of Ragnarök would be signaled by Fimbulwinter—three consecutive winters with no summer between them. The name means "mighty winter" or "great winter," and it would be exactly that: the winter that would not end, the cold that would break the world.

Snow would come from all directions. Fierce winds would blow constantly. The sun would provide no warmth even when visible. For three full years, the world would be locked in winter, with frost and ice spreading across lands that had once known growing seasons.

The first winter would bring hardship. Farming communities would struggle. Coastal settlements would face difficulties. Cities would suffer. But spring would be expected.

However, spring would not come.

The second winter without summer would bring worse suffering. Kinship bonds would break down. Brothers would kill brothers. Extended family networks would fail. Violence would increase as social bonds dissolved.

The third winter would see a complete breakdown of the social order. There was constant violence. The wilderness would overtake civilization. There would be moral disorder, and no one would trust each other. All oaths would be broken. The bonds holding society together would dissolve. Sacred spaces would be violated.

The realms beyond Midgard would feel Fimbulwinter differently. In Jötunheim, giants would watch and prepare. For them, endless winter was a sign their time had come, that the age of the gods was ending. Frost giants would thrive in the cold, growing stronger as their element dominated the world.

In Svartálfheim, dwarves in mountain halls might survive longer than surface dwellers. Deep underground, insulated by stone and with forge fires for warmth, they could endure. But even they would feel the shaking earth and would know something cosmic was breaking.

Álfheim and Vanaheim would suffer alongside Midgard. Light elves and the Vanir gods had their own harvests and stores, but three years without growing seasons would strain even divine resources. The Vanir, gods of fertility and growth, would feel the wrongness of this barren cold more acutely than most.

Asgard itself would feel doom's approach. Instead, the gods would watch Midgard suffering, knowing this heralded their own end. They prepared for war, knowing Ragnarök was coming. Odin gathered the Einherjar. Thor gripped Mjölnir tighter. The gods armed themselves and waited.

And then one day, the celestial order would break.

Two wolves had been chasing the sun and moon since the beginning. Their names were Sköll and Hati Hróðvitnisson. Sköll pursued Sól, the sun goddess, while Hati chased Máni, the moon god. Their chase had been eternal, lasting since the gods first set the sun and the moon on their courses. The wolves got close during eclipses but never caught their prey.

During Fimbulwinter, as foretold, the wolves finally succeeded.

Sköll caught the sun. The wolf's jaws closed around Sól's chariot and swallowed it. The light that had warmed the world since creation went out. The sky went dark.

Hati caught Máni moments later. The moon was swallowed. The pale light that had illuminated nights vanished.

Stars began to fall from their positions in the heavens. The constellations disappeared, and the sky became empty and dark.

The earth began to shake violently. Mountains trembled and cracked. Cliffs collapsed. The ground split open in places. Trees were torn from the ground. What buildings remained collapsed.

The great bindings were broken. In Jötunheim, on the island Lyngvi in Lake Ámsvartnir, Fenrir would feel Gleipnir weaken and snap. The ribbon that had held him since he bit off Týr's hand would break apart. The sword propping open Fenrir's jaws fell away. The wolf closed his mouth for the first time in ages, working his jaw. Then he opened his jaws wide—wider than before, wide enough to stretch from earth to sky. Fire burned from his eyes and nostrils as rage and hunger filled him.

The wolf shook himself, breaking free from the stone slabs and chains. He stood, massive beyond imagining, and began running toward the battlefield where the gods waited. Every step shook the ground. His howl echoed across all the worlds, announcing his freedom and coming revenge.

In the cave where Loki had been bound, the iron chains made from Narfi's entrails would crack and break. Loki would tear free, standing for the first time since his capture. The venom-dripping serpent above would fall as its magical binding failed. Sigyn would finally be able to set down the bowl she had held through Loki's entire imprisonment.

Loki emerged from the cave into the frozen, dark world. He stretched, feeling his freedom. Now he would lead armies against Asgard. Now he would help destroy everything the gods had built.

These signs were unmistakable. Everyone who survived—every god, every giant, every being across all the realms—knew that Ragnarök was here.

Ragnarök: The Twilight of the Gods

Heimdall stood at his post as watchman of the gods. He had been watching and waiting since the beginning, his keen senses alert for the first sign of Ragnarök. When Fenrir broke free and when the armies began marching, Heimdall saw.

He raised Gjallarhorn, the great horn that could be heard throughout all the Nine Worlds, and blew. The sound rang out—a clear, terrible note that announced the end had come. Every being who heard it knew what it meant. The final battle was beginning.

Yggdrasil, the World Tree, trembled. The ash tree holding the cosmos together shook from root to crown. Everything connected to it felt the shaking. The squirrel Ratatoskr stopped running up and down the trunk. The deer feeding on Yggdrasil's branches fled. Even Níðhöggr, the dragon gnawing at the roots, paused.

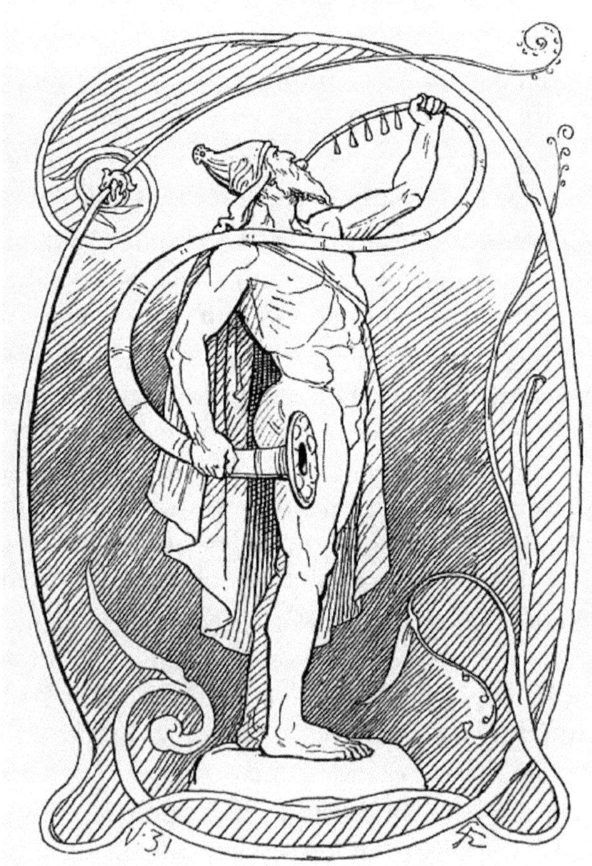

Heimdall blowing his horn.[15]

Odin rode to Mímir's well and consulted with Mímir's preserved head, seeking final counsel before battle. He then returned to Asgard, knowing what had to be done.

The gods armed themselves and gathered their forces. Odin wore his golden helmet and shining mail coat with Gungnir in his hand. The All-Father looked every bit the war leader he had always been, ready to lead his final charge. Thor had Mjölnir and his belt of strength, his iron gloves allowing him to wield the hammer. Týr prepared for battle despite having only one hand, his sacrifice to bind Fenrir about to come full circle as he faced monsters in the last fight.

Heimdall would join the battle after blowing his horn. Freyr looked at the weapons available and felt bitter regret; he had given away his self-fighting sword to win Gerðr's hand, and now he would face Ragnarök with an antler as his weapon.

The Einherjar poured out of Valhalla like a flood. Odin had been collecting these warriors since time began. These were men who had died bravely in battle, who had been chosen by the Valkyries, and who had spent every day since death training for this exact moment. They would march to Vígríðr, fight alongside the gods they had worshiped in life, and die in the greatest battle ever fought.

The march to Vígríðr, a vast plain where the final battle was to take place, was like nothing the Nine Worlds had ever seen. The gods rode at the front—Odin on Sleipnir, Thor in his goat-drawn chariot, the others on their mounts. Behind them came wave after wave of Einherjar, shields locked, spears bristling, war songs echoing across the frozen, dark landscape.

They marched through a world already dying. The darkness was total except for the light the army brought with them. Their torches, magical glowing weapons, and the radiance that still clung to some of the gods helped light the way. They marched over frozen ground that shook with earthquakes. They passed through ruins of Midgard, empty halls, and dead villages. They saw the corpses of Fimbulwinter's victims buried in the snow.

Vígríðr waited for them. This battlefield was enormous. The plain stretched a hundred leagues in every direction, according to the sources. It had to be that large to hold the armies that were gathering.

The giants came from Jötunheim. Frost giants and rock giants marched in massive columns, their footsteps making the ground tremble. These were beings the gods had fought for ages. They had been kept at bay, prevented from overrunning the ordered worlds. Now they were coming to finish what they had always threatened to do—destroy Asgard and everything the gods had built.

Hrym led them, a giant of enormous size carrying a shield as large as a house. The frost giants came from the east, their numbers beyond counting. Some rode on massive wolves. Others came on foot, each giant tall as a tree and strong enough to crack stone with their bare hands. They carried crude but effective weapons. Their clubs were made from tree trunks, their swords forged in giant smithies. Their axes could split mountains.

From Muspelheim in the south came Surtr and the fire giants. Surtr rode at their head, black as soot, wielding the flaming sword he had carried since before the gods existed. The fire giant had guarded Muspelheim's borders for all of time, waiting for this moment. Now he came north with all his people, bringing fire and destruction.

The sons of Muspell rode behind him—fire demons and burning giants, creatures of pure flame that scorched the ground wherever they stepped. Their presence made the frozen air hiss and steam. Fire and ice would meet at Vígríðr, the two primal forces clashing in the final battle.

Loki came from the east, commanding a ship. Naglfar sailed toward Vígríðr, though there was no water beneath it—perhaps it sailed through the air or perhaps over the frozen sea. This was the ship that had been built from the fingernails of the dead. It carried armies of the dead from Helheim, pale shadows given strength by Ragnarök's magic.

Loki stood at the helm, steering toward the battle. The gods had bound him and tortured him for ages. Now he came to take revenge. Hel, his daughter, sent her forces with him. These were the dead who had died from sickness and old age, from accidents and wounds, all rising to fight against the living gods.

From Niflheim came Garmr, the great hound who had guarded the entrance to Helheim. His chains had broken when all bonds failed. Now he ran free, his howl echoing across the frozen darkness, announcing death unleashed.

Fenrir ran alongside the armies, his massive form visible even in the darkness. His jaws were described poetically as stretching from earth to sky—his upper jaw scraped the heavens while his lower jaw dragged the frozen ground. Fire burned from his eyes and nostrils. The wolf ran toward Vígríðr, toward the gods who had tricked and bound him.

Jörmungandr, the World Serpent, came ashore, leaving the ocean for the first time since Odin had thrown it into the sea. The serpent's massive body churned the frozen waters as it crawled onto land. Venom sprayed from its fangs, poisoning the sky wherever the drops fell. The earth trembled under the serpent's weight as it slithered toward the battlefield, ready to face Thor one final time.

The two armies faced each other across Vígríðr. On one side were the gods, the Einherjar, and whatever forces of order remained. On the other side were the giants, fire demons, the dead, and monsters. The armies that met there were the largest ever assembled, gathering every force of chaos and destruction against the gods' final stand.

The battle began.

Odin rode straight toward Fenrir. Although the All-Father faced the wolf that prophecy said would kill him, he did not let that stop him from acting. He charged with Gungnir raised, leading his warriors into battle one last time.

Fenrir saw him coming and ran to meet him. The wolf's jaws gaped wide, fire burning in his eyes, every ounce of rage from his long imprisonment fueling his attack. Odin thrust with Gungnir, striking at the wolf's throat. The spear pierced Fenrir's flesh, but the wolf was too massive, too strong, too filled with hate to be stopped by one spear thrust.

Fenrir's jaws closed on Odin. The All-Father disappeared into the wolf's mouth. Fenrir's jaws snapped shut, and Odin was gone. The leader of the Æsir, the god who had created the world from Ymir's corpse, who had given breath to the first humans, who had ruled Asgard since the beginning, was dead, swallowed whole by the wolf he had once imprisoned. The Einherjar saw their leader fall and roared in fury and grief.

Fenrir had no time to savor his victory. Víðarr, Odin's son, saw his father die. He rushed toward Fenrir, wearing the special shoe he had prepared for this moment—a boot made from every scrap of leather ever discarded by shoemakers throughout time. All those bits trimmed from shoes, all those strips cut away and thrown aside, had been gathered and forged into this one massive boot.

Víðarr placed this boot against Fenrir's lower jaw. The wolf tried to bite, but Víðarr's boot held the jaw down, the accumulated leather of all the ages proving stronger than the wolf's bite. Víðarr grabbed Fenrir's upper jaw with his hands, gripping the massive fangs, and pulled.

He tore Fenrir's jaws apart. Víðarr avenged his father within moments of Odin's death, but the All-Father was still gone. The gods had to fight without their king.

Thor strode toward Jörmungandr with Mjölnir in hand. The god and the serpent had met before, when Thor fished for it and lifted it disguised as a cat. Now they faced each other for the last time. Both knew how this would end.

The serpent struck first, lunging with fangs dripping venom. Thor dodged sideways, swinging Mjölnir in a massive arc. The hammer crashed into the serpent's head with the sound of thunder. Jörmungandr recoiled. It was stunned but not killed.

Thor's fight with Jörmungandr.[16]

They fought across Vígríðr, god and serpent trading blows. Thor's hammer struck again and again, crushing scales and breaking bones. The serpent wrapped its coils around Thor, trying to crush him, but the god's strength was too great. He broke free and struck again.

Thor raised Mjölnir high and brought it down with all his divine strength directly onto Jörmungandr's skull. The hammer struck with the force of lightning. The serpent's head shattered. The World Serpent that had encircled Midgard since the beginning of time fell dead, its massive body convulsing as life left it.

But while the great serpent lay dying, its venom struck Thor. Poison sprayed from Jörmungandr's fangs, drenching the thunder god. Venom filled Thor's lungs, burned his skin, and coursed through his blood. Thor staggered back from the serpent's corpse, poisoned beyond healing. Nine paces from the monster he had slain, Thor fell.

Freyr faced Surtr across the battlefield. The Vanir god who had given up his sword for love now held only an antler as his weapon. Surtr advanced with the flaming sword that had burned since before creation, a weapon that could cut through anything.

Freyr fought bravely. He wielded his antler with skill, using his knowledge of combat to try to compensate for his inferior weapon. He dodged Surtr's massive swings, struck at vulnerable points, and used every trick he had learned in warfare. But an antler against a flaming sword was no contest.

Surtr's blade struck the god down. Freyr fell, killed by the enemy he might have defeated if he had still had his self-fighting sword. His choice to trade his sword for love cost him his life in the final battle.

Týr faced Garmr, the great hound from Helheim. The one-handed god of war met the monster with a sword in his remaining hand and courage that never faltered. Garmr leaped at him, jaws wide, larger than any wolf of Midgard.

They fought with savage intensity. Týr swung his sword, cutting at the hound. Garmr bit and clawed, trying to tear the god apart. Týr's missing hand made him vulnerable. He had no shield, no second weapon, nothing to defend his left side. But he fought anyway, striking blow after blow.

Finally, Týr's sword found Garmr's throat. He drove the blade home, killing the hell-hound. But in the same moment, Garmr's jaws closed on Týr. The hound's dying bite killed the god. Týr and Garmr fell together.

Heimdall and Loki met on the battlefield, two ancient enemies facing each other for the last time. They had history. Loki had stolen Freyja's necklace, Brísingamen, and Heimdall had pursued him and recovered it. They had fought then, transforming into various shapes, with Loki trying to escape and Heimdall refusing to let him. Now they would finish what they had started ages prior.

They fought with weapons and with cunning. Heimdall struck with his sword, while Loki dodged and countered. They were both skilled and clever fighters, and both were determined to kill the other.

Their battle was fierce and relatively even. Neither could gain a decisive advantage. They circled each other, struck, parried, and struck again. Blood was spilled on both sides. Finally, almost simultaneously, they delivered killing blows to each other.

Heimdall's sword pierced Loki's chest, and Loki's weapon struck Heimdall's heart. They fell together, the watchman and the trickster, dying in each other's arms. Neither would see what came after Ragnarök. Neither would survive to witness the new world.

Across Vígríðr, the Einherjar fought giants, fire demons, and the dead. The chosen warriors of Valhalla, who had trained for this moment their entire afterlives, threw themselves into battle with terrible joy. They died in their hundreds and thousands, but they took their enemies with them.

The battle raged across the enormous field. Gods fought monsters. Warriors fought giants. The Einherjar carved through their enemies like a blade, but there were too many foes. The forces of chaos outnumbered the forces of order. One by one, the defenders of Asgard fell. The battlefield became carpeted with corpses of gods, giants, warriors, and monsters.

Surtr, having killed Freyr, surveyed the battlefield. Almost everyone was dead or dying. The battle was nearly over. It was time to finish what had begun.

Surtr raised his flaming sword high above his head and swept it in a great circle. Fire flung from the blade in all directions. The flames consumed the bodies of the fallen, burning the blood-soaked ground of Vígríðr. Beyond the battlefield, the fire raced across the frozen landscape, melting snow and igniting anything that could burn. Trees caught fire and blazed like torches. The ruins of villages and cities burst into flame. Grass that had been buried under snow for three years ignited. Mountains caught fire, stone itself heating until it glowed. The frozen seas began to steam and boil as heat warped the water. Everything humans had ever built was consumed.

The fire reached Asgard. Valhalla, the great hall where the Einherjar had feasted and fought, caught fire and burned. The other worlds caught fire as well. Álfheim and Vanaheim burned. Svartálfheim's halls, deep in the mountains, filled with smoke and heat. Even Jötunheim, home of the giants who had helped cause this destruction, was consumed by Surtr's fire. The Nine Worlds all blazed together.

Yggdrasil, the World Tree, caught fire. Flames climbed its trunk, consumed its branches, burned through its leaves. The roots of Yggdrasil, deep in the earth, caught fire. The great tree that had stood since the beginning was consumed by flames.

Smoke from these countless fires rose and blackened the already dark sky. The air became ash and heat and death. Everything was burning. Everything was being destroyed.

As Yggdrasil burned and collapsed, the earth began to sink. The World Tree had held everything together, had provided the structure that kept the lands separate from the seas. Without it, the cosmic order failed completely.

Fire and water met as the burning earth descended into the sea. Steam rose in massive clouds as flames met water. The hiss and roar were deafening. The world was drowning and burning all at the same time, destroyed by fire from above and water from below.

The halls of the gods collapsed into ruins and slid beneath the waves. Asgard, the realm that had seemed eternal, fell into the sea, burning. Midgard sank, taking with it every trace of civilization. Jötunheim, Svartálfheim, Álfheim, and Vanaheim—all the worlds suspended in Yggdrasil's branches—fell as the tree collapsed.

The old order was destroyed, consumed by fire and drowned in water. Ragnarök—the twilight of the gods, the doom of the divine—reached its conclusion. The world as the Norse had known it was gone.

The Rebirth

After the fire died and the waters calmed, after the destruction was complete and the void had swallowed everything, something extraordinary happened.

The earth rose again from the sea.

Green and fertile land emerged from the waters that had drowned it. This was not the scorched, broken earth that had sunk—this was new land, fresh and clean, rising from the ocean like something being born. Grass grew on hills that had not existed moments before. Trees sprouted from soil that had never known roots. Meadows appeared, lush and green, untouched by fire or frost.

Waterfalls fell from cliffs, their waters clear and pure, unmarked by ash or blood. Rivers ran through valleys, fish swimming in their depths—new fish, or perhaps the descendants of those that had somehow survived in the deepest parts of the ocean. Eagles flew above the new lands, hunting, their cries echoing across mountains that had just risen from the sea.

Fields bore fruit without being sown. Grain grew wild, ripening under the light of the new sun. Berry bushes heavy with fruit appeared in clearings. The earth was young again, just as it had been in the beginning when the gods first created it from Ymir's body. The earth had been remade, given another chance, washed clean by the waters, and renewed.

Some gods had survived Ragnarök. Víðarr lived, having avenged his father Odin by tearing Fenrir's jaws apart. Váli, another of Odin's sons, also survived.

Móði and Magni, Thor's sons, survived as well. They searched through the ruins of the battlefield and found Mjölnir lying among the dead. Their father's hammer, the weapon that had defended Midgard for ages, that had killed countless giants and monsters, had survived the end of the world. Móði and Magni claimed it as their inheritance, taking up the hammer to wield in the new world.

And then Höðr and Baldr walked back from Helheim into the living world. Baldr, whose death had begun the sequence leading to Ragnarök, returned. The prophecies had foretold this. With the old world destroyed and the new world risen, Baldr could return to life. Höðr, Baldr's blind brother, returned with him so they could dwell together in the new world.

These surviving gods met at Iðavöllr, the field where Asgard once stood. They spoke about old times. They discussed the ancient wisdom, the knowledge that had been gained and lost, and remembered the gods who had fallen—Odin, who had led them; Thor, who had protected Midgard; Týr, who had sacrificed his hand; Freyr, who had given up his sword; and Heimdall, who had blown the final warning. They talked about the great events that had passed, the battles and betrayals and triumphs of the age that had ended.

As they spoke, they found golden gaming pieces in the grass. These were the pieces the Æsir had owned before Ragnarök, the games they had played when they were relaxing. Their presence suggested a connection between the old world and the new. It was evidence that not everything was lost.

The surviving gods would build again. They had Mjölnir. They had each other. They had a new, clean world to inhabit. They would create new halls, a new order, and new ways of living in a cosmos reborn. They had learned from the mistakes of the previous age. They had seen where pride, deception, and violence would lead. Perhaps they would do better this time.

From Hoddmímir's wood, two humans emerged. The forest had somehow survived the destruction, or perhaps it was newly created as a refuge. Either way, it had sheltered two people through Ragnarök: a man named Líf ("Life") and a woman named Lífþrasir ("Life-Yearner" or "Eager-for-Life").

They had hidden in the forest during Ragnarök's fire and flood. Now they came out into the new world. They saw green fields, a clean sky, waterfalls, and mountains. They saw a world empty of other humans, fresh and new, waiting for life to fill it again. They would be the new beginning of humanity.

Líf and Lífþrasir would have children, and those children would have children. This new generation of humans would spread across the new earth, building new settlements and creating new societies. Humanity was being given another chance, a fresh start in a world unmarked by the sins and sufferings of the previous age.

The sun returned to the sky. Before she was swallowed by Sköll, Sól had given birth to a daughter. This daughter now traveled the paths her mother had taken, illuminating the new world. The sky had a sun again, marking the days and seasons.

A new hall appeared in a place called Gimlé. It was described as fairer than the sun and roofed with gold. This was a place where righteous people would dwell. Another hall stood in the Nida Mountains, made of red gold, where beings called the Sindri dwelt. The existence of both halls suggested that the new world would have multiple dwelling places for the righteous.

However, the sources also mention Náströnd, "Corpse-Shore," a hall far from the sun. This hall was woven from serpents, with venom dripping from its roof like rain. Oath-breakers, murderers, and those who seduced other men's wives would have to wade through streams of that venom. A dragon called Níðhöggr, who had gnawed at Yggdrasil's roots in the old world, fed on the corpses there.

This detail is important. Even in the new world, there would be consequences for evil actions. The renewed cosmos was not a paradise where all wrongdoing would be forgiven or impossible. People could still choose to break oaths, murder, and betray.

Would this new world eventually face its own Ragnarök? Would the cycle repeat, with another Fimbulwinter, another final battle, another destruction and rebirth? The *Völuspá* ends with the image of the new earth rising green from the sea and the dragon Níðhöggr flying over the land, leaving the question of what comes next unanswered.

Some scholars interpret this as a cyclical pattern. Creation and destruction would repeat forever. Others read it as a single event, a unique transformation from the old world to the new, with no further repetition. The sources neither confirm nor deny that Ragnarök could happen again.

Ragnarök is a story about endings and beginnings, about destruction that makes room for renewal, about death that is followed by life. The new world rising from the sea was hope. Not naive hope that everything would be perfect and not false hope that suffering was over forever, but genuine hope that after the worst destruction imaginable, life could still continue and find a way to grow and thrive.

That was the true message of Ragnarök. The end is terrible, inevitable, and absolute. But it is also not permanent. After the twilight would come a new dawn.

Chapter 7: Living with the Gods

Blood and Fire: The Blót Ceremonies

Every autumn, when harvests were gathered and winter approached, communities across Scandinavia held ceremonies called *blót*. These weren't quiet prayers or contemplative rituals. Blót meant sacrifice, and sacrifice meant blood.

The word itself comes from a root meaning "to strengthen" or "to worship through sacrifice." At a blót, animals, like horses, cattle, pigs, and goats, were killed. Their blood was collected in bowls and then sprinkled on altars, on the participants, and on the walls of sacred spaces. The meat was cooked and eaten in communal feasts. This was how Vikings fed their gods and maintained the relationship between the human and divine worlds.

Blót ceremonies happened at specific times of year. The three major blóts were held at different points: one in autumn after harvest, asking for peace and good seasons; one at midwinter during Yule, for good crops in the coming year; one in spring, for victory and success, described in later tradition as the Sigrblót (victory sacrifice).

These weren't optional community gatherings. Adam of Bremen, a Christian chronicler writing in the 11th century, described a temple at Uppsala in Sweden where sacrifices occurred at major festivals associated with the number nine, which he reports took place every nine years and involved rites lasting multiple days. Nine males of every living creature were sacrificed, and their bodies were hung in a grove near the temple. Dogs, horses, and men all hang from trees as offerings to the gods.

Modern historians treat Adam's account cautiously, though, since he did not witness the rites himself.

Archaeological evidence confirms that animal sacrifice was widespread. Ritual deposits of animal bones appear at sites across Scandinavia. Horse bones are particularly common. Horses held special significance. They were valuable animals, so sacrificing them meant giving up something that mattered to the Vikings.

Adam of Bremen claimed human sacrifice happened. Some sagas mention it. Bog bodies and unusual burials found by archaeologists mostly predate the Viking Age and cannot be taken as direct evidence of Viking-period sacrifice. Vikings believed sacrifices worked. Giving the gods valuable offerings—animals, precious objects, and maybe even human lives—maintained the cosmic order and secured divine favor.

Who performed these sacrifices? In early Viking society, chieftains acted as priests. The same man who led warriors in battle and judged disputes would also conduct the blót, killing the animals and speaking the words that consecrated the sacrifice to Odin, Thor, or Freyr.

Later, especially in Iceland, a specific role developed: the *goði* (plural *goðar*). These were priest-chieftains who maintained temples, conducted sacrifices, and held both religious and political authority. The goðar weren't full-time priests in the Christian sense. They were wealthy farmers who had additional responsibilities in sacred matters.

The feasting after sacrifice mattered as much as the killing. Everyone ate the sacrificed meat together. This wasn't just a meal. It was communion with the gods, who were thought to participate invisibly in the feast. Sharing consecrated meat bound the community together and connected them to divine powers. Refusing to eat at a blót was a serious offense, as it was seen as a rejection of the community and its gods.

Toasts were drunk to the gods during these feasts. Someone would stand, raise a horn of mead or ale, and dedicate it to Odin for victory, Thor for protection, or Freyr for fertility and good seasons. Everyone would drink, passing the horn around.

Christianity ended the blót. As Scandinavia converted through the 10th and 11th centuries, Christian kings and missionaries forced people to stop sacrificing to the old gods. Temples were destroyed or converted to churches. The goðar either converted and became Christian leaders or lost their authority. After the Althing's (Iceland's national parliament—the oldest parliament in the world) decision around the year 1000 to adopt

Christianity, public pagan sacrifice was officially prohibited in Iceland, though sources report that some people continued private sacrifices for some time afterward.

Swearing by the Ring: Oaths and Honor

In Viking society, your word was quite literally sacred. Oaths were binding contracts witnessed by gods and enforced by supernatural power. Breaking an oath brought divine punishment, social destruction, and damnation after death.

The most solemn oaths were sworn on rings. These were not just any rings. These were sacred objects kept in temples or by goðar specifically for oath-taking. They had been consecrated to the gods, usually Thor or Ullr (most popularly known as the god of skiing, but he was also a god of oaths). When you swore on a ring, you weren't just making a promise to another person. You were calling the gods themselves to witness and enforce your words.

The ring-oath worked like this. Someone—usually a goði or chieftain— would hold out the consecrated ring, which some Icelandic sources describe as having been associated with sacrificial rites. You would place your hand on it and speak your oath aloud, invoking the gods by name. Everyone present heard the words. The gods, invoked by name and by the sacred object, were now bound up with your promise. If you broke the oath, you violated your agreement with the divine.

What happened to oath-breakers? In the myths, they ended up in Náströnd, wading through rivers of venom in the afterlife. In life, oath-breaking meant social death. Your word became worthless. No one would do business with you, fight beside you, or marry into your family. You became an *útlagi*, or an outlaw (literally "outside the law"). Anyone could kill you without legal consequences.

The sagas are full of people forced into exile or killed because they broke oaths. When a man swore to support his chieftain and then betrayed him, that betrayal was seen as a violation of the sacred order. Revenge wasn't just permitted; it was expected, even required.

Oaths bound people together in networks of loyalty. Warriors swore oaths to their leaders, promising to fight for them and share in their victories. Leaders swore oaths to their warriors, promising to reward loyalty and protect their people. These mutual oaths created the social structure of Viking warbands and societies.

Marriage involved oaths. When families arranged a marriage, both sides swore oaths guaranteeing the terms, including the bride price, the dowry, and the rights of children. These oaths, witnessed by the community and the gods, made the marriage legitimate and binding.

Blood brotherhood was established through oath-taking. Two men who weren't related by blood could become brothers through a ritual that involved mixing blood and, in some accounts, walking under an arch of turf while swearing oaths. Once made, these bonds were supposed to be as strong as family ties. Odin and Loki's blood brotherhood was the mythological model for this practice.

Legal disputes were resolved through oaths. If you were accused of a crime, you could swear you were innocent. However, the oath had to be backed up by oath-helpers—other people willing to swear that your word was good. If you couldn't find oath-helpers willing to vouch for you, your oath meant nothing. The system assumed that honest people would have friends willing to back them, while liars and criminals wouldn't.

The weight of an oath varied by the person swearing. A powerful chieftain's oath had more legal weight than a poor farmer's oath. But everyone's oath had some weight, and the gods were thought to punish oath-breakers regardless of social status.

Runes were sometimes carved on oath rings or on objects related to oath-taking. These runes invoked divine power and made the oath even more binding. A ring with Thor's name in runes was an especially powerful object for oath-swearing because the god's name was literally present in the sacred object.

Christians tried to maintain the oath system when Scandinavia converted, but they replaced the sacred rings and invocations of Thor with crosses and invocations of Christ. The structure remained—oaths were still sworn on holy objects and witnessed by the divine—but the divine power being called on changed.

The Skald's Craft: Keeping the Gods Alive in Verse

Skalds were not merely entertainers. They were living memory, political weapons, and repositories of sacred knowledge, all compressed into one person. A skilled skald could make or destroy reputations, preserve history, and invoke the gods through the power of carefully crafted words.

Skalds performed poetry with force and precision. Their verses were meant to impress people, challenge ideas, and preserve information.

Skaldic poetry was incredibly complex. Unlike modern poetry, which tends toward simplicity and emotional directness, skaldic verse was deliberately intricate. Skalds used kennings, or compressed metaphors in which one thing stood for another. "Wound-giver" meant sword. "Odin's drink" meant poetry, referencing the Mead of Poetry. "Horse of the sea" meant ship.

But kennings went deeper. A skald could use a kenning within a kenning. "Feeder of the raven of the goddess of the necklace" meant "warrior." Work it backward. The goddess of the necklace is Freyja, who owned Brísingamen. Her raven is a battlefield scavenger, and someone who feeds ravens is a warrior because he creates corpses for them to eat. All of that was compressed into a few words.

Why did the Vikings make poetry so complicated? It was partly to show skill—anyone could string together simple words, but only a master could craft intricate verses that still followed strict meter and alliteration patterns. But there was more to it. The complexity itself had power. Working through a kenning required you to know the myths. "Odin's drink" only makes sense if you know the story of the Mead of Poetry.

Skalds performed at feasts, particularly after blót ceremonies. A chieftain would host a feast, and his skald would compose verses praising the chieftain's generosity, bravery, and victories to enhance the chieftain's reputation. In a world without mass media, your reputation was what people said about you, and what skalds composed about you became the permanent record.

Insult poetry was equally powerful. A skald could destroy someone through verse. If a skald composed poetry suggesting a man was cowardly, sexually weak, or dishonored, that poetry would spread. Other skalds would repeat it, and people would remember it. The victim's reputation would be ruined.

Because of this power, some societies banned certain types of insult poetry. Icelandic law specifically forbade níð poetry—verses designed to damage someone's honor. The punishment for composing níð could be exile or death because the damage it caused was considered serious.

Skalds also served as historians. They memorized genealogies—who descended from whom, going back generations to divine or heroic ancestors. They preserved stories of past battles, great deeds, and important events. This oral preservation was how Viking history survived.

Learning to be a skald took years. You had to memorize vast amounts of existing poetry, learn the complicated meter patterns, and master the hundreds of kennings and their variations. Apprentice skalds studied under masters, practicing composition and performance until they could create professional-quality verse.

Skalds were primarily men. Women could be skalds too, though the sources preserve far fewer names of female poets. Some women composed poetry at funerals, praising the dead and lamenting their loss.

The best skalds were paid well. A chieftain would grant land, ships, or treasure to a skald who composed particularly impressive praise poetry. Some skalds traveled from court to court, composing for different leaders and accumulating wealth through their art.

However, skalds also took serious risks. If you composed praise for a chieftain, and he failed (if he lost a battle or died dishonorably), your reputation suffered too. If you composed insult poetry, your target might kill you.

Christianity changed skaldic practice. Christian skalds composed about Christ and the saints rather than Odin and Thor. The kennings were adapted. "Son of Mary" replaced "son of Odin." But the basic techniques survived. The complexity, the alliteration, and the emphasis on craft all persisted even after the content shifted from pagan to Christian.

Until the conversion, though, skalds were among the primary figures who kept the gods alive in daily life. Elite feasts and major gatherings often included skaldic performance. Through their intricate, powerful verses, the myths were living knowledge, constantly renewed and reinforced through poetic craft.

Death in the Real World: Viking Funeral Practices

While the myths describe Valhalla and Helheim, actual Vikings had practices for dealing with their dead. Archaeology has revealed elaborate burial customs showing what people believed about death and the afterlife.

Ship burials were among the most spectacular Viking funeral practices. The deceased would be placed in a ship along with grave goods, and the ship would either be buried in the ground or burned on land in a cremation rite. The famous ship burials at Oseberg and Gokstad in Norway show this practice in detail.

The Oseberg burial, discovered in 1904, contained a large ship buried in a mound. Inside were two women, along with an enormous array of grave goods, including wooden carts, sleighs, textiles, tools, kitchen equipment, and animal bones. The burial included at least fourteen or fifteen horses (sources vary), along with dogs and other animals. The ship itself was beautifully built and decorated. The burial dates to around 834 CE.

The Oseberg ship.[17]

One of the buried women was possibly a queen, and the other was perhaps a servant buried to accompany her. The grave goods demonstrate enormous wealth and status. The ship burial practice itself indicated beliefs about the deceased needing a vessel for a journey to the afterlife.

The Gokstad ship, discovered in 1880, contained a single male burial with a different array of grave goods. The ship was larger and more robust than the Oseberg ship, as it had been built for ocean voyages. The man buried there had weapons, horses, dogs, and exotic birds, demonstrating both wealth and far-ranging trade connections.

These ship burials weren't common. They were elite burials for people of extremely high status. Most Vikings received simpler burials.

Cremation was also widely practiced. The deceased would be burned on a pyre, often with possessions. The ashes and remaining bone fragments were then placed in an urn and buried or scattered, depending on local practice.

Ibn Fadlan, an Arab traveler who encountered the Vikings on the Volga River in 922 CE, wrote a famous account of a ship cremation he witnessed. He described an elaborate funeral for a Rus' chieftain that involved the sacrifice of a slave woman to accompany the chief, and the burning of both bodies along with the ship and grave goods. The entire ship was consumed by fire.

Ibn Fadlan's account is valuable but also problematic. He was an outsider observing practices foreign to him, and his description was filtered through his own cultural assumptions. However, it remains one of the few contemporary written descriptions of a Viking funeral and describes practices that align with archaeological evidence in some respects.

Grave goods varied widely depending on the deceased's status, gender, and occupation. Warriors were buried with weapons, including swords, axes, spears, and shields. Women of high status were buried with jewelry, textile tools, and household items. Craftspeople had tools of their trade. The contents of graves reflect a person's role in life and what people believed they might need after death.

Animals accompanied many burials. Horses were particularly common in high-status graves. Dogs were also frequent.

Burial mounds marked many graves. These could range from small earth mounds to enormous structures that dominated the landscape. The mounds served as memorials, marking the deceased's graves and announcing their importance to passersby. Some mound fields contained dozens of burials.

Stones were another burial marker. Stones arranged in ship shapes, circles, or other patterns surrounded graves. These stones marked the space as sacred to the dead.

The practice of placing the dead in boats or ship-shaped stone settings was connected to beliefs about journeys to the afterlife. The ship represented transportation to another realm—sailing to Hel's kingdom or Valhalla or some other destination.

What's notable is the variation in burial practices across Viking Age Scandinavia. Different regions had different customs, and practices changed over time. There wasn't one standard "Viking funeral" but rather a range of practices that shared some common elements while differing in details.

The arrival of Christianity complicated burial practices. Christian burials required different orientations, different grave goods or none at all, and different rituals. As Scandinavia converted to Christianity through the 10th and 11th centuries, burial practices shifted. We can observe this archaeologically in changes in grave styles and contents.

Some burials from the conversion period show mixed practices. For instance, a grave could have a Christian orientation with pagan grave goods or be a pagan burial mound with Christian crosses. This indicates a transitional period in which people hedged their bets or maintained old customs while adopting new ones.

Conclusion

Christianity came, converting Scandinavia gradually from the 8th through the 12th centuries. This conversion took time. For several generations, people wore Thor's hammer amulets alongside crosses. They kept old customs while adopting new ones. When Christianity became dominant, temples were destroyed and official practices were stopped, but many Norse traditions survived as folk belief for centuries, transforming into folklore rather than disappearing overnight.

The written myths survived too, preserved by Christian monks and scholars.

Why would Christians preserve pagan myths? Some saw value in recording the past as history. Some thought understanding the old religion would help them convert people. Some were interested in poetry, and the myths were essential to understanding traditional Norse poetry.

The most important figure was Snorri Sturluson (1179–1241), an Icelandic scholar who wrote the *Prose Edda* around 1220. It is our most important source for Norse mythology.

Snorri was a Christian writing for Christians, but he knew mythological knowledge was essential for understanding poetry. His *Prose Edda* is structured as a handbook for poets, including *Gylfaginning* (the systematic account from creation to Ragnarök) and *Skáldskaparmál* (detailed explanations of poetic language).

Writing in 13th-century Iceland, two centuries after conversion, Snorri captured a fading tradition. The old religion was gone, but the stories persisted in poetry and cultural memory. He wrote them down; however, as a Christian explaining a dead religion, his interpretations sometimes tell us more about medieval Christian thinking than about authentic Norse belief. He also claimed that the Norse gods were historical figures later mistaken as gods, which made the myths more acceptable to Christian audiences.

Snorri saved a lot, but his work is an edited selection. Many myths and deities remain just names without stories. Gods like Ullr or Sága are mentioned in sources but have almost no narratives attached because Snorri didn't know them or chose not to record them. We have only a fraction of what once existed.

The *Poetic Edda* survives in manuscripts from the same period, though the poems themselves are older. They were composed in the Viking Age, passed down orally, and eventually written by Christian scribes.

The written sources come through Christian filters. They are stories told by pagans, remembered through the generations, and then recorded by Christians. However, archaeology allows us to verify the written accounts. Amulets, picture stones, burial sites, and other physical evidence confirm some mythological elements while complicating others. Iceland played a special role too. It was settled late and converted peacefully in 1000, creating conditions in which old stories could be valued as heritage rather than suppressed as heresy.

To put it simply, we're lucky to have these myths at all.

Modern Echoes

These ancient myths haven't stayed in the past. They've shaped modern culture in ways the Norse couldn't have anticipated.

J. R. R. Tolkien drew heavily on Norse mythology for Middle-earth. The dwarves in *The Hobbit* have names taken from the *Völuspá*—Thorin, Fili, Kili, and others. Gandalf's name comes from the same list. The concept of Middle-earth itself echoes Midgard. Richard Wagner's *Ring* cycle operas drew on the *Völsunga Saga* and Eddic poems. Marvel Comics turned Thor and Loki into superheroes, introducing them to massive audiences. Modern fantasy as a genre owes enormous debts to Norse mythology. Different races, world trees, and magic runes can all be traced to these sources.

But why do these stories still resonate with us today? Part of the answer is the gods themselves. They're flawed, mortal, and make mistakes. They face unsolvable problems and know their doom is coming. Modern readers find these imperfect gods more accessible than all-powerful immortals.

The inevitability of Ragnarök resonates strongly. The Norse faced their doom with courage rather than despair. This speaks to modern anxieties about climate change, instability, and existential threats. The Norse model offers comfort. You do what's right, not because you'll win, but because it's right.

There's also something honest about the Norse acceptance of destruction. Unlike myths in which good triumphs permanently, Norse mythology says everything ends. But then the world is reborn. Something new emerges from the ruins. This cyclical view feels realistic. Things do end, but life continues.

The complexity appeals too. Loki is a blood brother to Odin but constantly causes problems. He's neither purely villain nor purely trickster. Thor is strong but not always smart. Odin pursues wisdom but makes questionable choices. These aren't simple characters with clear moral alignments.

The myths offer vivid imagery: Yggdrasil connecting worlds, Thor fishing for the serpent, Odin hanging on the tree. The stories are exciting, dramatic, and full of stakes and consequences. They deal with fundamental questions—why are we here, what happens after death, how should we face suffering—in ways that engage imagination and emotion.

These myths survived the death of the religion that created them. They survived being written down by Christians who didn't believe them. They survived a thousand years of copying and retelling. The Norse gods lost to Christianity, but the stories didn't die. And that's what matters. These ancient myths still help us understand life, death, and what it means to face the inevitable.

Here's another book by Matt Clayton that you might like

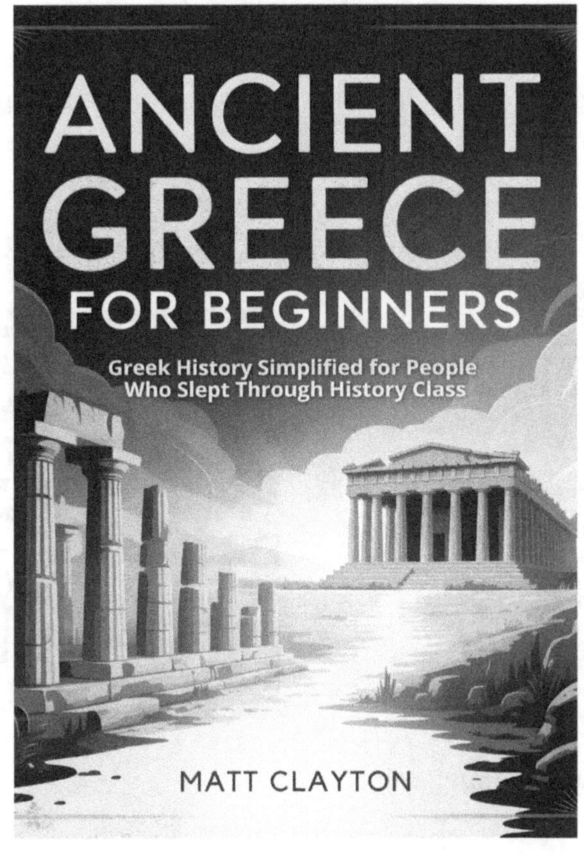

Free Bonus from Captivating History (Available for a Limited time)

Hi History Lovers!

Now you have a chance to join our exclusive history list so you can get your first history ebook for free as well as discounts and a potential to get more history books for free!

Simply visit the link below to join.

Or, Scan the QR code!

captivatinghistory.com/ebook

Also, make sure to follow us on Facebook, X, and YouTube by searching for Captivating History.

Sources and References

Abram, Christopher. *Myths of the Pagan North: The Gods of the Norsemen.* London: Continuum, 2011.

Davidson, H. R. Ellis. *Gods and Myths of Northern Europe.* London: Penguin Books, 1964.

Gunnell, Terry. *The Origins of Drama in Scandinavia.* Cambridge: D. S. Brewer, 1995.

Larrington, Carolyne, trans. *The Poetic Edda.* 2nd ed. Oxford: Oxford University Press, 2014.

Lindow, John. *Norse Mythology: A Guide to the Gods, Heroes, Rituals, and Beliefs.* Oxford: Oxford University Press, 2002.

McKinnell, John. *Meeting the Other in Norse Myth and Legend.* Cambridge: D. S. Brewer, 2005.

Orchard, Andy. *Dictionary of Norse Myth and Legend.* London: Cassell, 1997.

Price, Neil. *The Viking Way: Magic and Mind in Late Iron Age Scandinavia.* 2nd ed. Oxford: Oxbow Books, 2019.

Simek, Rudolf. *Dictionary of Northern Mythology.* Translated by Angela Hall. Cambridge: D. S. Brewer, 1993.

Sturluson, Snorri. *Prose Edda.* Translated by Anthony Faulkes. London: J. M. Dent, 1995.

Turville-Petre, E. O. G. *Myth and Religion of the North: The Religion of Ancient Scandinavia.* London: Weidenfeld and Nicolson, 1964.

Image Sources

1   https://commons.wikimedia.org/wiki/File:AM_738_4to_Yggdrasill.png

2   https://commons.wikimedia.org/wiki/File:Ask_and_Embla_by_Robert_Engels.jpg

3   https://commons.wikimedia.org/wiki/File:The_Wolves_Pursuing_Sol_and_Mani.jpg

4   https://commons.wikimedia.org/wiki/File:Georg_von_Rosen_-_Oden_som_vandringsman,_1886_(Odin,_the_Wanderer).jpg

5   This file is licensed under the Creative Commons Attribution 4.0 International license, https://commons.wikimedia.org/wiki/File:Tj%C3%A4ngvide_bildsten_-_Historiska_museet_-_108203_HST_-_14081_(cropped).jpg

6   https://commons.wikimedia.org/wiki/File:M%C3%A5rten_Eskil_Winge_-_Tor%27s_Fight_with_the_Giants_-_Google_Art_Project.jpg

7   Ola Myrin, Statens historiska museum/SHM, CC BY 4.0 <https://creativecommons.org/licenses/by/4.0>, via Wikimedia Commons, https://commons.wikimedia.org/wiki/File:Claes_Kurck_Sk%C3%A5ne_hammer_-_HST_DIG55488_original.jpg

8   https://commons.wikimedia.org/wiki/File:Louis_Huard_-_The_Punishment_of_Loki.jpg

9   Nils Asplund, CC BY-SA 3.0 <https://creativecommons.org/licenses/by-sa/3.0>, via Wikimedia Commons, https://commons.wikimedia.org/wiki/File:Nils_Asplund_-_Heimdal.jpg

10 Ronny Ueckermann, CC BY-SA 4.0 <https://creativecommons.org/licenses/by-sa/4.0>, via Wikimedia Commons, https://commons.wikimedia.org/wiki/File:Historiska_museet_043.jpg

11 I, Berig, CC BY-SA 3.0 <http://creativecommons.org/licenses/by-sa/3.0/>, via
Wikimedia Commons, https://commons.wikimedia.org/wiki/
File:U_240,_Lingsberg.JPG

12 https://commons.wikimedia.org/wiki/File:Ah,_what_a_lovely_
maid_it_is!_by_Elmer_Boyd_Smith.jpg

13 https://commons.wikimedia.org/wiki/File:Baldr_dead_by_Eckersberg.jpg

14 https://commons.wikimedia.org/wiki/File:Loki,_by_M%C3%A5rten_
Eskil_Winge_1890.jpg

15 https://commons.wikimedia.org/wiki/File:Heimdallr_by_Froelich.jpg

16 https://commons.wikimedia.org/wiki/File:Thor_und_die_Midgardsschlange.jpg

17 Petter Ulleland, CC BY-SA 4.0 <https://creativecommons.org/licenses/by-sa/4.0>, via
Wikimedia Commons, https://commons.wikimedia.org/wiki/
File:Osebergskipet_2016.jpg